The Solution is Full Reserve /

100% Reserve Banking.

Ralph S. Musgrave.

Merton Miller (economics Nobel Laureate) on Irving Fisher's 100% reserve banking proposal:

"Think how much national economic welfare could rise under Fisher's narrow banking scheme when thousands of no longer needed bank regulators (and hundreds of academic banking economists) find themselves forced at last to seek more socially productive lines of economic activity."

Milton Friedman on why full reserve has never been adopted:

"The vested political interests opposing it are too strong, and the citizens who would benefit both as taxpayers and as participants in economic activity are too unaware of its benefits and too disorganized to have any influence."

Martin Wolf: "..under current arrangements, banking institutions create the vast bulk of the money in our economy as a byproduct of often irresponsible risky lending. Since people view money as the one safe asset, this has to be a fundamentally crisis-prone, system. It could be replaced, at least in theory, by returning the ability to create money to the state."

This work is an updated version of a paper with the same title and published on the Munich Personal Repec Archive site.

Table of contents.

Summary

Section 1 of this work argues the case for full reserve banking. Section 2 explains the flaws in a large number of arguments put AGAINST full reserve, and section 3 explains the flaws in a few arguments put IN FAVOUR of full reserve.

This book is a slightly updated version of an online paper with the same title. The main changes / improvements are to section 1.4.

Abbreviations.

FDIC. Federal Deposit Insurance Corporation. FDIC is a self-funding insurance system for small banks in the US.

FR. Full Reserve Banking.

MCC. Money Creation Committee.

MMT. Modern Monetary Theory.

MPC. Monetary Policy Committee (of the Bank of England).

NSI. National Savings and Investments (a UK government run savings bank).

PM. Positive Money.

QE. Quantitative easing.

TBTF. Too Big to Fail.

Section 1: Introduction to full reserve banking.

1.1 Full reserve banking in brief.

The term full reserve (FR) refers here to the system advocated by the following, amongst others.

1.Laurence Kotlikoff, economics professor in Boston. See Kotlikoff (2012, p.43). However, for a quick introduction to Kotlikoff's ideas see Klein (2013).

2. Richard Werner, economics professor in Southampton, UK. See Werner (2011). Incidentally the online version of the latter work says on the first page that the work is dated. I beg to differ: if you want a CONCISE summary of Werner and co-authors' ideas, this work is a good starting point. Obviously for more detailed, and I think minor subsequent variations, then look at the authors' later works.

3. Milton Friedman. See Friedman (1960, Ch3, starting at heading entitled "Banking Reform").

4. James Tobin, economics Nobel Laureate. See Tobin (1985 & 7).

5. Merton Miller, economics Nobel Laureate and co-author of the "Modigliani-Miller" theory.

6. Ben Dyson, founder of Positive Money. See Dyson (2012).

7. John Cochrane, economics professor in Chicago. See Cochrane (2013).

8. Irving Fisher, professor of political economy at Yale in the early 1900s. See Fisher (1936).

FR is sometimes called "100% reserve banking". This is a very brief thirty five word summary of FR, (in bold italics).

The bank industry is split in two. One half offers totally safe accounts where money is simply lodged at the central bank. The other half offers normal bank loans, but that half is funded only by shares.

As for a longer summary (about 1,400 words), that is as follows.

The existing banking industry is split in two. One half offers depositors accounts which are totally safe (or as near total safe as it is possible to get). And that safety is not achieved by any sort of artificial taxpayer funded subsidy for banks as is the case with safe accounts under the existing system. Under FR, safety derives from the fact that the money concerned is GENUINELY SAFE. That is, relevant sums are not invested in anything the least risky: the money is just lodged at the central bank. But possibly (as advocated by Friedman) some money is invested in short term government debt. Thus "safe" money earns little or no interest, but IT IS instant access.

The second half of the industry lends to mortgagors, industry and so on. But that half of the industry is funded just by shareholders, or stakeholders who are in effect shareholders. Or as Irving Fisher (1936) put it, "each commercial bank would be split into two departments, one a warehouse for money, the checking department and the other the money lending department...."

Each advocate of FR has slightly different ideas as to how to design an FR system. For example under Kotlikoff's system, both halves of the industry consist of mutual funds ("unit trusts" in the UK), with the first or safe half consisting of money market mutual funds that place money only at the central bank (and possibly also invest in government debt) and the second half consisting of non-money market mutual funds which lend to mortgagors, businesses and so on. And those with a stake in non-money market mutual funds are in effect shareholders, in exactly the same way as those with stakes in existing non-money market mutual funds are in effect shareholders, though they are not normally referred to as such.

As to Friedman's system, there again, the entities making up one half of the former banking industry are separate from the entities making up the second half. In contrast, under Werner's system, safe accounts and accounts which lend on account holders' money are offered under the same roof. However, the basic principle behind each variation on the FR theme is the same.

The two halves of the industry will be referred to below as the "safe" and "lending" halves.

As to what reserves the lending half should have under FR, there is no good reason for it having ANY, as is already the case for banks in several countries (though those banks do maintain a small stock of reserves so as to enable them to settle up with each other). Thus the phrase "full reserve" is a bit of misnomer in that half the banking industry under FR might have almost no reserves. But like many misnomers in English and other languages, the phrase has established itself.

Stimulus.

As to how stimulus is implemented under FR, that can be done in at least three different ways.

1. Interest rate adjustments.

2. As advocated by Werner (2011) and Dyson (2012), it can be done by adjusting the amount of base money created and spent by the state, and/or adjusting taxes. That is, the amount that state spends net of tax collected can be adjusted.

As for who decides what amount of stimulus is suitable at any point in time, the conventional view is that stimulus should be decided by some sort of independent committee of economists: the Bank of England Monetary Policy Committee being an example of a committee of that sort, which has decided on interest rate adjustments for many years.

In similar vein, Werner and Dyson advocate that in the case of adjusting government net spending, that should be decided by a committee like the MPC. Note that such a committee (as in the case of the existing MPC) would decide PURELY how much stimulus was suitable. That it is, the committee WOULD NOT intrude on POLITICAL questions, like what proportion of GDP to allocate to public spending any more than the existing MPC intrudes in that way.

As to the relative merits of adjusting interest rates versus adjusting government net spending, that is discussed in section 1.6 below, and the conclusion is that Werner and Dyson are correct: that is, interest rate adjustments are a poor way of regulating demand.

3. For those who do not like allegedly "undemocratic" committees, like existing central bank committees or Werner and Dyson's proposed "Money Creation Committee", having POLITICIANS determine stimulus is always a possibility. Thought the dangers of allowing politicians access to the printing press are widely appreciated, which is why a majority of economists and others are not keen on the idea.

The basic rule of FR.

The basic rule governing FR can actually be reduced to about 10 words, as follows (in bold italics).

"All lending entities above some minimum size must be funded just by shareholders".

That rule necessarily implies that entities which accept deposits which are supposed to be totally safe cannot lend (other than, as per Friedman's suggestion, lend to government).

Anyone aware of the fact that simple rules (like E-MC^2 in physics) may be of fundamental importance, should have their interest in FR aroused by the above ten words. That is in contrast to the Byzantine complexity and questionable effectiveness of existing attempts at bank regulation, like Vickers (2011) in the UK or Dodd-Frank in the US.

To summarise, those who want their money loaned on or invested under FR carry the full costs or risks involved. That would tend, firstly to raise interest rates, second to cut total loans and debts, and in consequence, the total amount invested would decline a bit. The cut in investment might seem to be a weakness in FR. However, note that interest rates rise ONLY TO THE EXTENT THAT a subsidy of the bank industry or lending industry has been removed. And since subsidies distort markets and reduce GDP, the removal of the latter subsidy would INCREASE GDP, rather than reduce it. But there is more on that point below.

Would very high capital ratios do?

An alternative to FR is to implement a big rise in capital ratios, but not to the 100% level. That would certainly be a big improvement on the existing system. However, the rise in capital ratios has to be sufficiently large that governments are happy to remove ALL BANK SUBSIDIES, and that includes, 1, lender of last resort, 2, depositor insurance, and 3 the TBTF subsidy. Subsidies misallocate resources and reduce GDP.

So far, governments are NOWHERE NEAR removing all bank subsidies. Thus far higher capital ratios are needed, if not the full 100% ratio. But, 100% is a clear line in the sand: anything less will probably just result in banks bribing and cajoling politicians in the future into gradually reducing the ratio to around the ridiculously risky 3% that obtained just before the recent crisis. Also, as is shown below (section 1.4) there are no real costs involved in a 100% rather than a 50% or 30% ratio. Reason is the Modigliani Miller theory. Thus the 100% ratio makes sense.

And quite apart from Modigliani Miller, there is a glaring flaw in the idea that funding a corporation of any sort mainly via shares rather than short term debt raises funding costs to any great extent: that is the fact that many stock exchange quoted corporations are funded mainly by shares, e.g. the oil company, BP.

The advantages of FR are:

1. No more bank failures. No bank or lending entity can SUDDENLY fail in the way banks have failed regular as clockwork over the centuries. In contrast, a SLOW DECLINE of a lending entity / bank under FR is perfectly possible, resulting perhaps in a takeover by a stronger entity. The reason banks cannot fail under FR is as follows.

As to safe entities / accounts, the money there is near completely safe. And as to lending entities, if lending is done in an incompetent manner, all that happens is that the value of the relevant shares (or mutual fund units) falls: the actual entity does not become insolvent.

As George Selgin put it in his book on banking, Selgin (1988), "For a balance sheet without debt liabilities, insolvency is ruled out...". (Incidentally, that was an aside made by Selgin: his book did not actually advocate FR).

2. Improved stability. A second advantage of FR is that the above stability of lending entities / banks reduces the severity of the boom bust cycle. There is more on that point in Section 2.32 below.

3. Bank subsidies vanish. The near impossibility of bank failures means that the TBTF and other bank subsidies can be removed under FR.

4. Depositor / investors choose. Under FR, depositor / investors HAVE A CHOICE as to what is done with their money. That is in contrast to the existing system where so to speak, banks can use grandma's saving to bet on risky derivatives. Given the latter choice, the large majority of former bank depositors would probably opt for something conservative, like having their money fund safe mortgages (e.g. mortgages where householders had a minimum 20% or so equity stake). And that ought to reduce the amount of irresponsible lending.

5. No limit to deposit guarantees. There is no need under FR to limit deposit guarantees, as pointed out by Dyson (2012). That is, there is no need to limit to the amount of money that households or firms can keep in a totally safe manner. That is in contrast to the existing system where governments usually guarantee the safety of only a limited amount of money per person (£85,000 in the UK at the time of writing).

The reason for that limit is that under the existing system, government (i.e. taxpayers) run a GENUINE RISK under the latter £85,000 type guarantee because the money is GENUINELY not entirely safe. In contrast, under FR, money in safe accounts really is safe, thus there is no reason for £85,000 type limits.

Also, the deposit guarantee is only available to INDIVIDUAL PEOPLE in some countries. There is no reason for not allowing FIRMS to have a totally safe method of storing money in any quantity they want.

1.2   More on the deposit guarantee.

There are two apparent weaknesses in the latter points on deposit guarantees. **First**, in the UK, depositors can actually lodge up to £1million with total safety at National Savings and Investments (a government run savings bank) which reduces the relevance of the above merit in FR in the case of the UK. However, that £1million type facility is not available in EVERY country.

Second, it could be argued that anyone with more than about £85,000 in spare cash is rich enough to look after themselves, thus the "no limit" as under FR is not a huge advantage. On the other hand £85,000 is only about a third the cost of the average house in the UK at the time of writing. Thus anyone selling a house or small business before buying a replacement runs the risk of losing a huge sum if a bank collapses before the new house or business is bought. So the "no limit" characteristic of FR is a definite advantage.

Incidentally, selling a house before buying a replacement is not uncommon and can make sense, if the seller can find somewhere to live in the interregnum relatively easily (maybe rented accommodation or living with relatives). Having a pile of cash puts them in a good bargaining position when it comes to buying the replacement house.

1.3 Defects in recent attempts at bank regulation.

Several authorities have pointed to the very defective nature of recent attempts to improve bank regulation. The following are a sample.

1. Article by Britain's former prime minister, Brown (2013), entitled "Stumbling Towards the Next Crash". The title says it all.

2. The main British investigation into banks was conducted by the so called "Vickers Commission": see Vickers (2011). For a scathing indictment of the Vickers report, see Kotlikoff (2012).

3. The former head of the UK's Financial Services Authority, Turner (2014), said: "…already agreed reforms to financial regulation, though undoubtedly valuable, are inadequate to prevent a future repeat of a 2007-8 style crisis."

4. The main US proposals for bank reform are in the so called "Dodd-Frank" act. John Cochrane (2013) started his paper with the words, "In recent months the realization has sunk in across the country that the 2010 Dodd-Frank financial-reform legislation is a colossal mess."

5. Article by Schiller (2014) entitled "The Financial Fire Next

Time".

6. On the subject of Dodd-Frank, Richard Fisher, President of the Dallas Federal Reserve Bank said, "We contend that Dodd–Frank has not done enough to corral "too big to fail banks" and that, on balance, the act has made things worse, not better." (Fisher (2013)).

In contrast to the latter criticism of Dodd-Frank by Fisher, Krugman (2014b) claims Dodd-Frank has substantially reduced the TBTF subsidy. But even if Krugman is right, that still leaves several banking problems which are solved by FR but not by attempts at reform to date, like Dodd-Frank.

1.4 Doesn't a 25% or so capital ratio bring near total safety?

FR imposes a 100% capital requirement on lending entities / banks, with a view, amongst other things, to making them failure-proof. But it might seem that a capital requirement of around 25% as advocated by Admati (2013) and by the chief economics commentator at the Financial Times, Wolf (2012), makes it near impossible for lending entities to fail, plus that can be backed up with FDIC type bank insurance to ensure that in the event of failure, depositors do not lose out. In fact the arguments for "25% plus FDIC" are flawed, and for numerous reasons as follows.

a) Assets can fall more than 25%. In the case of small banks in the US, it is far from unheard of for their assets to fall to below 75% of liabilities, and in that case a 25% capital ratio is clearly inadequate. Doubtless the chance of assets falling in value that far in the case of a large bank are lower. But there are no sharp dividing lines here. That is it is common for assets to fall to a few percent below the value of liabilities in the case of large banks. (See Peston (2012) Ch 1, under the heading "False Optimism" on the precarious position of several large British banks in the 1970s, 80s and 90s.)

That is, rather than sharp dividing lines, it would be more accurate to say that there is a very real prospect of a bank becoming technically if not actually insolvent when the capital ratio is about 3%, while the chance of insolvency becomes vanishingly small as the ratio rises to 50% and 100%.

b) Taxpayer funded insurance is a subsidy. Some bank deposit insurance (e.g. in the UK) is taxpayer funded, and that's an obvious nonsense, because it is a subsidy of banks. In contrast, a self-funding FDIC bank insurance system at least has the merit of not being subsidised by taxpayers.

c) Insurance does not cut irresponsibility. Insurance, even when it is self-funded, does not greatly reduce irresponsibility, and the irresponsibility shown by bankers in recent years has been disgraceful. Reason is that as with any insurance system, if you know that given irresponsibility, the "insurance company" pays, then there is little incentive to behave responsibly. In contrast, under FR, where irresponsible loans are made, it is PURELY those funding the relevant loans who foot the bill. That reduces irresponsibility, while of course not eradicating it.

d) Insurance does not influence total costs. Having the

capital ratio a bit on the low side and dealing the consequent risk for depositors with FDIC self-funded insurance does not make sense. Reasons are as follows.

Suppose the chance of a bank failing to the extent of wiping out depositors is 1% in any given year and that that is the only risk. The appropriate premium would obviously be 1% of total deposits. But if as an alternative, there is NO DEPOSIT INSURANCE, then depositors will want a bigger return, and to cover the risk they run, they'll demand an extra 1%. Thus as far as costs of funding the bank go, there is no difference between those two scenarios.

Nor is there any difference between those two scenarios for depositors. In the more risky scenario (25% with no FDIC) depositors earn 1% more (because they do not have any insurance premium to pay for) but there's a 1% chance per year of their losing all their money. That is the same as earning 1% less with no chance of losing their money.

In short, once all state or taxpayer funded support for banks is removed, the concept "depositor" in the traditional sense (i.e. someone who is 100% sure to get their money back because of taxpayer funded guarantees) becomes a logical absurdity. So called depositors actually become shareholders, or at least shareholders OF A SORT. They might be something like preference shareholders or "bailinable" bond holders. But the latter two are nevertheless shareholders of a sort: they stand to make a loss if things go badly wrong.

Ergo the removal of bank subsidies leads automatically to a 100% capital ratio, at least in a broad sense of the phrase "capital ratio".

There are of course numerous different possible arrangements here. For example, apart from the ordinary shareholders who fund lending banks under FR, a portion of the funding could come from preference shareholders, bailinable bond holders or quasi-depositors. Dyson (2012) advocates the latter. But that raises the question as to what proportion of funding should come from ordinary shareholders vis a vis other types of "bank funder". This work does not claim to give a definitive answer to those sort of questions, but there is probably little difference in overall costs and benefits as between the different possible arrangements. (Various criticisms are made of Dyson's proposals in this connection in section 1.14 below). In contrast, the IMPORTANT and basic idea behind FR, and idea which brings BIG BENEFITS, is that lending banks should be 100% funded by shareholders or funders who are in effect shareholders.

Allow quasi depositors / preference shareholders?

One argument AGAINST allowing lending entities / banks to be funded by any sort of preference share or bailinable bond or quasi deposits is thus. Lending banks under FR arguably just become fund managers (as pointed out by Coppola (2014)). Now EXISTING mutual funds have not found it worthwhile splitting those who invest in such funds in ordinary shareholders and other types of stakeholder like preference shareholders. Thus it looks like mutual funds run by banks under FR would not find that split worthwhile either.

Moreover, if something like preference shares WERE ALLOWED, it would be important not to let them become too "money like". That is, the mere fact of allowing something like preference shares is to get onto a slippery slope which leads back down to the existing system under which the vast bulk of the country's money supply is issued by private banks and underwritten by taxpayers: and even THAT fails to prevent the occasional credit crunch, followed by years of excess unemployment.

Preventing preference shares, or something of the sort, becoming too money-like can of course be thwarted first by making it abundantly clear that there is no taxpayer backed guarantee for those shares and second by stopping instant access to those funds (as proposed by Dyson). Nevertheless, that slippery slope is always a danger.

Another argument against any sort of preference share or quasi depositor is thus. Traditional depositors (i.e. depositors protected by taxpayer funded guarantees) are certainly willing to lend to banks at a lower rate than shareholders. However, once that taxpayer funded support is removed, and it is made abundantly clear that there is no taxpayer funded guarantee behind those deposits, it is possible that that cheap source of funding for banks pretty much dries up. And that may well explain why EXISTING MUTTUAL FUNDS have not found it worthwhile splitting shareholders (as mentioned above) into ordinary shareholders and shareholders who are more in the nature of preference shareholders / depositors. Thus there may be little benefit to be derived from allowing quasi deposits / preference shares.

e) Corruption. Another argument against anything less than a 100% ratio for lending entities / banks is that if the capital ratio IS RAISED to just 25% (or any other non-100% level) banks will simply bribe and cajole politicians and regulators over the years into reducing the ratio back down to the 3% or so that has obtained over the last decade or so. In contrast, 100% is a clear line in the sand.

Indeed, George Osborne, Britain's finance minister, has campaigned against ANY IMPROVEMENT WHATEVER in the capital ratio. The fact that his political party, the Conservative party, is partially funded by banks is of course entirely coincidental. (See Wolf (2013)).

And on the subject of "bribes and cajoling" note that the British finance industry spends about £90m a year on lobbying politicians, according to Mathaison (2012), while in Europe as a whole, there are 1,700 lobbyists working for banks (Corporate Europe Observatory (2014)).

f) Any bank subsidy means capital ratios are too low.

Another argument for the 100% rather than 25% or so ratio is thus. Any claim (implicit or explicit) by regulators that they have raised capital ratios by enough while bank subsidies of any sort are still in place is a flagrant self-contradiction. And "bank subsidy" includes taxpayer funded deposit guarantees and lender of last resort. Subsidies misallocate resources: they lead to reduced GDP. Thus when the authorities can announce loud and clear that no support of ANY SORT is available to banks in ANY CIRCUMSTANCES, then and only then can they claim that capital ratios are high enough.

Now exactly what capital ratio will give the authorities the confidence to declare that no support of any sort is available for banks? Well, a 100% ratio would. As to a 50% ratio, it is hard to say. So a reasonable conclusion is: might as well go for 100%.

Conclusion so far. The question as to what extent we should allow lending entities / banks to be funded by bank creditors who resemble traditional depositors or preference shareholders is a complicated area, and this work does not claim to give a definitive answer to this question. However, there are certainly good arguments for keeping it simple: that is just having lending entities / banks funded by ordinary shareholders and forbidding anything that resembles traditional depositors. And that is the simple rule of thumb adopted in Milton Friedman and Laurence Kotlikoff's versions of FR.

g) Modigliani Miller. Another flaw in the idea that 25% maybe plus FDIC results in banks being funded more cheaply than in the case of 100% was set out by Franco Modigliani and Merton Miller (MM). As they explained, the relatively high return demanded by shareholders simply reflects the risks they run, plus the TOTAL RISK involved in funding a given bank is a given: it is FIXED. Thus if the risks are spread over a larger number of shareholders, there is no change to the TOTAL CHARGE that shareholders will make for covering those risks. In short, apart from the increase in bank funding costs that derive from the removal of bank subsidies, bank funding costs are not increased by raising the above 25% to 50% or even to 100%. (See Admati (2013b) for more arguments behind the latter point. Incidentally Admati certainly advocates much higher capital ratios, but she does not specifically advocate the 100% ratio far as I know.)

Bank funding cost increases due to subsidy withdrawal.

There is however one reservation to be made in connection with the MM claim that bank funding costs do not rise when capital ratios rise, and that is that as those ratios rise, bank subsidies are necessarily withdrawn. To illustrate, when the ratio is around 3% it is obvious to everyone that bank insolvency is a real possibility, plus it is obvious that when large banks are in difficulties, government will not let them fail. I.e. taxpayers are effectively carrying part of the risk. However, when the ratio rises to around 25% or higher, it is obvious that shareholders are carrying nearly all the risk. Thus given that rise in capital ratios, shareholders WILL DEMAND a bigger return on capital. But that simply reflects the withdrawal of a subsidy, and there is nothing wrong with that.

A second factor tending to raise the return demanded by shareholders, and which again amounts to nothing more than a reflection of the fact that a subsidy is being withdrawn is thus. To the extent that the supply of shareholders for the country as a whole is inelastic, a rise in capital required by banks will result in a rise in returns demanded by shareholders in all corporations (banks included) for the country as a whole. But to repeat, that simply reflects the removal of a subsidy, thus there can be no legitimate objections there.

Flawed Criticisms of Modigliani Miller.

As distinct from the latter "removal of a subsidy" reservations about MM, a number of allegedly more serious criticisms have been made of MM. In fact these criticisms are feeble, and the rest of this section is devoted to rebutting the most common of these criticisms. So readers not interested in this can obviously skip the rest of this section.

1. Tax. About the most popular criticism of MM has to do with the different tax treatment of bank capital and bank debt. At least that tax point is the first criticism cited by Elliot (2013), Miles (2011, p.9) and Vickers (2011 section 3.45), and it is only one of two criticisms cited by Ratnovski (2013) and the ONLY criticism cited by Kashyap (2010). Birchler (2012) also cites the tax point.

This tax criticism of MM is simply that if the tax treatment of bank capital and bank debt is different, then MM does not work out in the real world in the same way as it does in theory.

Answer. The very simple answer to that is that tax is an entirely ARTIFICIAL imposition. Thus for the purposes of gauging REAL costs and benefits, tax should be ignored. If a big tax was imposed on apples, and for no good reason, that would not mean that the REAL COST of producing apples had risen.

It is INCREDIBLE that the above six so called "authorities" who cite the tax criticism of MM have apparently not tumbled to the latter simple flaw in the tax criticism, but that seems to be the case. And if the latter tax criticism is the best that the critics of MM can do, then rest assured that the other criticisms (dealt with below) are near hopeless.

2. Different returns on capital and debt.

Ratnovski's only other criticism of MM, which he does not present with what seems a lot of confidence, is that assuming the return on bank capital is 15% and the return on bank debt is 5%, then the more capital there is, the higher the cost of funding the bank.

Answer. Well of course, but it's PRECISELY the latter sort of 15%/5% assumption that MM demolishes. Ratnovski's point there is a bit like saying "if the Earth was flat we would not have weather satellites".

3. Incorrectly priced deposit insurance.

The second criticism of MM made by Miles (2011) (also the second criticism made by Elliot (2013) is that the charge made for deposit insurance may not reflect the risk, in which case MM would not work out in the real world the way it does in theory.

Answer. The flaw in that argument is much the same as the flaw in the above "tax" criticism: for the purposes of gauging REAL costs and benefits, any "incorrect" or artificial charges should be ignored. That is, in such cost / benefit calculations or arguments, CORRECT OR ACCURATE charges should be assumed, even if those are not the charges that obtain in the real world.

And the latter policy is the one adopted in the rest of this work. For example bank subsidies are deplored in every other page of this work. And a subsidy almost by definition consists of a charge which OUGHT TO BE imposed on banks, but which is not, a classic example being deposit insurance enjoyed by UK banks which is funded by taxpayers rather than banks themselves.

4. Asymmetric information.

Elliot's third criticism (also made by Birchler (2012)) is that new share issues have to be offered at a discount because those buying shares do not have perfect information about what a bank does.

Answer. Exactly the same applies to bonds issued by a bank and to deposits. That is, depositors do not trust banks 100%, thus depositors "lend" less money to banks, and charge a higher rate of interest for doing so than if they had perfect information about the bank.

5. Regulators and banks do not agree on MM.

Birchler (2012) seems to think that the fact that banks and regulators do not agree on the relevance of MM is a weakness in MM. As he puts it in reference to MM, "Bankers and regulators thus fail to agree on the relevance of even the validity of a half-century old theorem."

Answer. This might be news for Birchler, but cops and robbers often disagree! In fact it is not unknown for them to employ extreme violence against each other. And if there is any doubt that banks are robbers, remember that they have been fined around $100bn in the US recently. Yes that's billion, not million.

6. Bank shareholders want leverage.

Another feeble point made by Birchler is that bank shareholders want leverage. As he puts it, "Firstly, once a bank is already leveraged, shareholders are tempted to push leverage further leverage".

Answer. Well of course they will. Pickpockets, if they were as brazen as bankers, would be "tempted to push for" the right to pick pockets.

7. State guaranteed deposits.

Birchler's next criticism of MM is that banks do not need more capital because they can fund themselves from taxpayer backed deposits. As he puts it "..banks can raise insured deposits (or liabilities with implicit state guarantee)."

Answer. Well of course, but taxpayer backed deposits are a subsidy of banking! Hopefully readers will forgive me if I ignore the rest of Birchler's article. It is clearly a waste of ink and paper.

8. Banks will increase risks.

Elliot's fourth criticism is that higher capital ratios, improve bank safety, which may induce banks to take bigger risks.

Answer. The WHOLE POINT of raising capital ratios is to prevent banks offloading risk onto taxpayers. And if banks find they cannot unload that risk, i.e. have to carry the risk themselves, they are almost bound to become more cautious or responsible, rather than (as suggested by Elliot) take bigger risks.

If the state guaranteed to replace my car if I write it off in an accident, that is an inducement to irresponsibility on my part. If I then have to insure it myself, assuming there is a significant no claims bonus, then I will drive more responsibly.

But if by any chance higher capital ratios DID RESULT in increased risks, why should we care? As long as the risk is taken by shareholders rather than taxpayers, then that is free markets working in the way they should. Oil companies take big risks when drilling for new oil deposits: sometimes there is no oil there. That is how capitalism and free markets work.

The beauty of a bank that is funded just by shareholders is that if risks do not pay off, it cannot go insolvent, which disposes of systemic risks, as pointed out above.

9. The transition to full reserve.

Elliot's fifth criticism is that the transition to higher capital ratios may involve problems, and that banks may react to higher capital requirements by cutting lending rather than actually acquiring more lending.

Answer. The "transition" point is addressed in section 2.9 below. As for the possibility that banks will react to higher capital requirements at least to some extent by cutting lending, that is not a possibility: it's a certainty, as pointed out in section 1.9. To reiterate the point made in 1.9, higher capital requirements reduce the extent of bank subsidies which in turn raises interest rates which cuts total debts and lending.

Elliot claims that "If banks do cut back on credit provision, then either the economy is likely to be slowed down, or less regulated entities will pick up the lending slack, bringing up other risks that will be covered in the next section." The answer to that (as pointed out in 1.9) is that higher capital requirements involve removing or reducing subsidies and subsidies misallocate resources, i.e. reduce GDP. Thus far from less lending causing a REDUCTION in GDP, as claimed by Elliot, the actual effect would be to INCREASE it.

10. Shadow banks.

Elliot's final criticism is that increased capital requirements will drive business to the shadow bank sector. That point is dealt with in section 2.15 below.

Conclusion. People who think up simple and profound new ideas, like $E=MC^2$ or the Modigliani Miller theory are often followed by lesser mortals, who come in two forms. First those who try to jump on the "new idea bandwagon" by suggesting minor changes to the new idea. Second there are nit pickers who try to find fault with the new idea. The above criticisms of MM are in the nit picker category.

1.5 The inherent defect in privately created money.

Money has taken many forms thru history: gold coins, tally sticks and so on. Nowadays nearly all money is a liability of banks: commercial banks and central banks. To be more accurate, money is certainly a liability of a commercial bank, while the extent to which money is a liability of a central bank is more debatable – (see section 2.2 below).

So money is a debt owed by a bank, plus it is a debt that is more or less fixed in value (inflation apart). That is, $100 buys about the same selection of goods in a week's time as it buys today.

But the glaring problem with an entity that has liabilities that are fixed in value and assets that CAN FALL in value (e.g. when unwise loans are made) is that when the assets DO FALL in value, the relevant entity / bank is on its way to insolvency or is actually insolvent. And the brute fact is that banks have failed regular as clockwork throughout history.

That problem can be solved by having government (i.e. taxpayers) stand behind commercial banks. But that amounts to a subsidy, and subsidies are frowned on in economics, and quite right: unless there is some very good justification for subsidies, they reduce GDP.

Another alternative is some sort of self-funding insurance for banks, but that has problems which are explained in section 1.4 above.

However, FR disposes of bank liabilities that are fixed in value: the only liabilities (if you can call them that) on the balance sheet of a lending entity under FR are shares, which by definition and in practice vary in value by significant amounts.

So is the abolition of privately created money a problem? Not at all: because (as mentioned above) CENTRAL BANKS ALREADY ISSUE a form of money. Thus there is nothing to stop central banks supplying ALL MONEY, or whatever amount of money is needed to keep an economy working at capacity.

Bitcoin changes value.

An obvious exception to the idea that money is not money if it changes significantly in value is Bitcoin, which has changed value dramatically in recent years. The answer to that is that Bitcoin types of money will never take off in a serious way, at least in that the vast majority of individuals and firms are not interested in seeing the contents of their bank accounts suddenly halve in value.

Moreover, it is totally unrealistic to think that that the US government will let any Bitcoin type system displace the US dollar, and same goes for other countries. Bitcoin has already been banned in Russia.

1.6   Interest rate adjustment is a defective tool.

As pointed out above, two leading advocates of FR (Dyson and Werner) claim that the best way to regulate demand and inflation is by adjusting the amount of new base money created and spent. Or the alternative for those who do not want a bigger public sector is to cut taxes while leaving public spending unchanged (or reduced), and as to the "tax shortfall" that would cause, that can be made good by simply creating new base money.

That is not to suggest that a net increase in the money supply is suitable in EVERY YEAR: in particular, given an outburst of Alan Greenspan's "irrational exuberance" there would be the occasional year in which a net REDUCTION in the money supply would be suitable so as to calm things down. But certainly, the 2% inflation target (assuming it is achieved) cuts the value of the supply of base money in REAL TERMS every year, so newly created money is needed to make up for that. Plus economic growth reduces the value of the money supply RELATIVE TO GDP, and that reduction will tend to need countering. So all in all, a significant annual increase in the money supply in terms of dollars / pounds / euros, etc will normally make sense.

In short, the state has to increase the amount of base money every year ANYWAY: i.e. even if interest rate adjustment is better as a fine tuning device. As to the conventional wisdom, namely that interest rate adjustments should be one of the more important tools when it comes to adjusting demand, there is actually a VERY LONG LIST of problems involved in interest rate adjustments as follows.

1.   Distortion.   Interest   rate   adjustments   are DISTORTIONARY. An interest rate change works only via households or firms which are significantly reliant on variable rate loans. I.e. those reliant on FIXED rate loans or not reliant on loans at all are not directly affected by an interest rate change. Thus interest rate changes affect one set of households and firms, but not another set. So to that extent, interest rate adjustments make about as much sense as any other distortionary method of adjusting demand you care to think of: e.g. boosting an economy only via people with black hair, with blondes, red-heads, etc waiting for a trickle-down effect.

A possible answer to the latter point, is the common claim that TAXES are also distortionary. And that is of relevance here because in the case of the Werner / Dyson "adjust government net spending" system, one way of adjusting government net spending is to adjust taxes. The suggestion that taxes are distortionary is a popular one: the suggestion was put for example by Bullard (2011) and Wren-Lewis

(2014b).

However, there is a simple answer to the above "distortionary taxes" point which is that clearly taxes CAN BE distortionary: e.g. a tax on red cars but not cars with a different color. On the other hand a flat percentage tax on everyone's income would be almost completely distortion free.

2. Availability of credit. The idea that there is a close relationship between interest rates and the ACTUAL availability of credit is VERY QUESTIONABLE given that between around 2010 and 2014, interest rates were at record lows but banks were reluctant to lend.

3. Empirical evidence. A recent study done by the Federal Reserve (Sharpe (2014)) found little relationship between interest rates and investment spending.

4. Bubbles. Interest rate reductions can cause asset price bubbles.

5. Market forces. The price of borrowed money should, at least on the face of it, be determined by the same system that determines the price of coal, oil, steel and a million other commodities: supply and demand. That is there are good reasons, set out in the economics text books, for thinking that GDP is maximised where prices are set at market prices (except where there are strong social reasons for thinking otherwise).

Thus if the state interferes with the free market rate of interest, then on the face of it, the total amount invested will not be optimum and GDP will not be maximised.

6. Investors look at the long term. Low interest rates allegedly encourage investment. Unfortunately those making investments look at LONG TERM rates, not the fact that the central bank has recently cut rates and will probably raise them again in two years' time. And that applies both to borrowing by firms and by households.

While most people will not buy houses just because interest rates have dropped for a couple of years, there ARE those NINJA mortgage incompetents who bought houses on the basis of near zero interests for the first year or two. I.e. there ARE incompetents out there. So in that the "low interest rates encourages investment" argument DOES WORK, it works at least partially by encouraging incompetents to be incompetent: not a ringing endorsement for the "low interest rates encourage investment" argument.

7. Investment not needed in recessions. The idea that reduced interest rates encourage investment is rendered near irrelevant by the fact that in a recession, more investment is exactly what is NOT needed. In recessions (certainly in SHORT recessions) there is more than the usual amount of capital equipment lying idle! Of course it takes TIME to manufacture or create real investments like machinery or factories, and assuming an economy will return to trend growth shortly after a recession, employers need to make sure they are not SHORT of capital equipment after a recession. But employers do not need governments to tell them this. Nor will irrelevant little inducements like 2% changes in interest rates do much to optimise any given employer's investment strategy.

8. Radcliffe Report. The Radcliffe investigation into

monetary policy in the U.K. published in 1960 concluded that 'there can be no reliance on interest rate policy as a major short-term stabiliser of demand'.

9. Credit cards. Credit card interest rates are not influenced by base rates. See UK CreditCards.com (2009) and Insley (2011).

10. Keynes. Keynes said, "I am now somewhat skeptical of the success of a merely monetary policy directed towards influencing the rate of interest...it seems likely that the fluctuations in the market estimation of the marginal efficiency of different types of capital...will be too great to be offset by any practicable changes in the rate of interest." Keynes's General Theory – near the end of Ch 12.

11. Lags. It is sometimes argued that monetary policy (interest rate adjustments at any rate) can be made quickly, i.e. fiscal changes take longer to implement.

That point is irrelevant. The IMPORTANT question is TOTAL TIME LAG between the decision to implement a policy and the actual effect.

An article entitled "How Monetary Policy Works" (Bank of England (no date given)) estimated the maximum effect of interest rate adjustments came after about ONE YEAR. In contrast when it comes to tax rebates, Johnson (2006) found that, nondurable consumption increased by about two thirds of the rebate during a six-month period (close to 40 percent during the three-month period of the rebate, and the remaining in the following three months). So on that basis, there is no huge difference between lags in the case of monetary and fiscal policy: in fact fiscal policy looks like being slightly better.

Also, in that increasing government net spending consists of expanding the PUBLIC SECTOR, the effect ought to be pretty well IMMEDIATE. That is, if government decides to hire additional people, the effect comes just as quickly as people can be interviewed, and hired.

12. Borrowing from abroad. The objective in raising interest rates is to cut demand in the country concerned. Unfortunately raising interest rates induces foreigners to buy government debt. But that temporarily boosts the value of the country's currency on foreign exchange markets. And that is just an uncalled for or "nuisance" effect. That is exports and importers are inconvenienced and for no good reason.

13. Fiscal versus monetary policy. There is disagreement amongst economists as to how effective monetary and fiscal stimulus is. That problem can be solved by doing both at once: that is, simply creating new base money and spending it, and/or cutting taxes.

If one policy is much more effective than another, it doesn't matter: the COMBINATION is guaranteed to have an effect.

14. Galbraith. J.K.Galbraith said (correctly): "firms borrow when they can make money, not because interest rates are low". And that intuitive point is backed by evidence: see Schoder (2013).

15. Interest rate adjustments promote inequality. In order to adjust interest rates at all, there must be a stock of government debt on which interest is paid. And to achieve that, the state must issue debt (forgive the statement of the obvious). But what is "government debt"? Well it's simply a liability of the state. But the state already issues a liability of a sort, namely base money.

So in order for there to be government debt, the state must issue what might be called an "excessive" stock of liabilities. That is, it must issue not just the stock of base money that gives us full employment: it must issue so much that the private sector has to be induced NOT TO SPEND the excess by lending it back to government (at interest).

But it is taxpayers that fund that interest and a significant proportion of taxpayers are on average incomes or less, while those with an excess stock of base money will tend to be the better off. Thus the set up required to enable interest adjustments to be used to influence demand is one that promotes inequality!

16. Central banks. It could be argued that where a boom is caused by additional investment spending (some of which will inevitably be funded by more borrowing), having the central bank raise interest rates is the suitable tool for countering such a boom.

The first answer to that is that in practice, central banks do not make much of an effort to work out the cause of booms and confine interest rate rises just to cases where the boom is caused by increased investment. Put that another way, central banks do not, given a CONSUMER led boom, try to persuade the fiscal authorities (i.e. the rest of the government machine) to impose deflationary measures of a fiscal nature (i.e. reduce public spending or tax increases).

Second, even to the extent that central banks DO COUNTER investment led booms with interest rate rises, that "countering" will not be successful to the extent that investment is funded out of retained earnings and share offerings.

17. Wren-Lewis. One argument put for interest rate adjustment, rather than adjusting the amount of base money and put by Wren-Lewis (2013) is essentially that raising the amount of base money will raise demand and/or inflation expectations, which in turn is inflationary, which in turn reduces the real rate of interest, which in turn raises demand. Ergo, so the argument goes, raising the amount of base money is not necessary because the latter cut in real interest rates saves the day.

Well the simple answer to that is that the latter additional inflation will not take place unless the increase in base money has a demand and/or inflation increasing effect. Thus the cure for the problem (inadequate demand) comes about as a result of the increase in base money BEFORE the cut in the real interest rates comes about!

Incidentally, Wren-Lewis argued that point in relation to an increase in the stock of base money that stems (in real terms) from the Pigou effect rather than from a DELIBERATE increase implemented by the state and consisting of an increase in that stock in NOMINAL terms. But that makes no difference to the basic argument.

18. Werner. For more arguments and evidence on the deficiencies of interest rate adjustments, see Werner (1997).

1.7 It is not just FR advocates who want to vary the amount of base money created and spent.

Regulating aggregate demand by adjusting the amount of new base money created and spent (net of any change to taxes) rather than regulating demand via interest rate adjustments is not an idea supported just by advocates of FR. In fact several countries during the 2008-14 recession put the latter idea into effect on a large scale in that they implemented fiscal stimulus and followed that with QE. The reasons why fiscal stimulus plus QE comes to the same thing as "create and spend" are set out in the paragraph in italics just below.

Also, advocates of Modern Monetary Theory tend to back the create and spend idea, as does Hillinger (2012): see his p.3, paragraph starting "An aspect of...". Also Wren-Lewis (2014) advocates the idea, at least near the zero bound.

Why "create and spend" equals fiscal stimulus plus QE.

Assume "fiscal stimulus" consists of government borrowing $X, spending $X and giving $X worth of bonds to those it has borrowed from. If the central bank then prints $X and buys back those bonds, that all comes to the same thing as the state printing $X and spending it. The only slight difference is that under the former, the central bank is left holding $X of bonds. But that simply amounts to one arm of government (the central bank) being owed $X by the rest of the government machine, which is a bit like your right hand pocket owing money to your left hand pocket: meaningless.

1.8   New base money should be spread widely.

To repeat, the decision as to how to allocate new base money under Dyson and Werner's system is left to politicians, but there is the question as to whether that new money should be allocated to any SPECIFIC types of public spending or particular types of tax cuts (as advocated by Ryan-Collins (2013)). In fact there is a very good reason for NOT concentrating the extra spending or tax changes to specific areas to too great an extent. That is, in the case of extra spending, the new money should be spread fairly evenly over the economy as a whole and for the following very simple reason.

The amount of stimulus needed varies hugely from one year to the next. If stimulus money is all concentrated on say education, the result will be big gyrations on the total amount spent on education. And if there is one way of getting bad value for money from expenditure (public or private), it is to implement dramatic increases or reductions in such expenditure.

1.9   A bit less investment would not matter.

The word "investment" is imbued with near magical qualities for the unsophisticated, and the sophisticated know it and exploit the fact. For example Britain's former prime minister, Gordon Brown, regularly referred to CURRENT spending in the public sector as "investment" with a view to promoting public sector spending. No doubt that fooled a significant proportion of voters.

Investment also satisfies a primordial emotional craving: that's the idea that sacrifice (in this case sacrificing current consumption so as to fund investment) must bring benefits. That primordial emotion also explains the popularity of austerity: that is, "we spent excessively prior to the crisis, so that can only be put right by sacrifices to the Gods, aka austerity".

Anyway, moving on from caveman psychology to 21st century economics, there is a widely accepted principle in economics which is that subsidies do not make sense, absent a very good social reason for a subsidy. That is, subsidies misallocate resources, i.e. reduce GDP.

And FR removes the subsidies currently enjoyed by lenders, thus under FR interest rates would rise, thus there would be a decline in 1, the total amount loaned, 2, debts and 3, investment.

However, subsidising lenders in effect subsidises investment, that is, it leads to a more than optimum amount of investment. Thus FR in returning total mounts invested to something nearer the optimum ought to RAISE GDP, not reduce it.

Moreover, a relatively small proportion of investment is funded by bank lending. Reason is that banks lend to businesses for relatively short periods (at least in the UK) and have a habit of not rolling over, or renewing their loans. Investments in contrast last for a decade or more, thus it makes sense for a business to fund them out of retained earnings, shares and so on, rather than bank loans.

And finally, interest paid on the typical mortgage in the

1980s in the UK was up to THREE TIMES the rate typically paid at the time of writing. Yet economic growth was far better in the 1980s than during the last five years during which we have enjoyed the questionable advantages of record low interest rates, and that hardly supports the idea that high interest rates harm economic growth.

Conclusion. Investment (and debts) would decline under FR, all else equal, but the decline would be small, plus far from reducing GDP, the effect ought to be too INCREASE it.

1.10 FR is being imposed on MMFs in the US.

At the time of writing, the US Securities and Exchange Commission is trying to impose the rules of FR on Money Market Mutual funds, which casts doubt on any claims that FR is difficult or impractical. See Weiner (2014) and SEC (2014).

To be more exact, the SEC is going to forbid MMFs that invest in anything more risky than base money or government debt from promising depositors they will get $X back for every $X deposited. In contrast MMFs THAT DO invest in anything more risky will have to let depositors' stake in the MMF float in value along with the value of underlying assets. And that is FR, pure and simple.

To quote from SEC (2014), *"The SEC is removing the valuation exemption that permitted institutional non-government money market funds (whose investors historically have made the heaviest redemptions in times of stress) to maintain a stable net asset value per share ("NAV"), and is requiring those funds to sell and redeem shares based on the current market-based value of the securities in their underlying portfolios....*"

As to what the SEC calls "Government MMFs" (i.e. MMFs that lodge depositors' money in an ultra-safe fashion), they say:

"The fees and gates and floating NAV reforms included in today's Release will not apply to government money market funds, which are defined as a money market fund that invests at least 99.5% of its total assets in cash, government securities..".

There is of course an anomaly here which is that FR is being imposed on MMFs but not on regular banks. And given that there is not a big difference between the two, those running MMFs may well try to use their political connections to have the SEC's proposals reversed.

Another "FR compliant" development is that the New Zealand Labour Party is contemplating giving their central bank a say on fiscal stimulus, which looks very much like the "create base money and spend it" policy advocated by some advocates of full reserve. See O'Brien (2014).

1.11 Benes and Kumhof's debt jubilee.

An IMF working paper, Kumhoff (2012) advocated FR but included a HUGE debt jubilee in the process of converting to FR. That is not necessary: that is, the arguments for and against debt jubilees are entirely separate from the arguments for and against FR. So why did Kumhof combine the two?

The answer is that IT MIGHT SEEM that it is not possible to dispose of the sort of debt based money created by commercial banks without disposing of the relevant debt. That is not true. To illustrate, gold coins (so called "sovereigns") were used as money in the UK in the 1800s, but they went out of use. But that did not mean that the actual gold disappeared.

Same applies to debt. Debt CAN BE used as money, but ceasing to use it in that way and adopting some other form of money does not mean the relevant debt necessarily vanishes. The way to achieve a "jubilee free" conversion to FR is set out in section 2.42 below.

1.12 FR forces banks to find savers before loans are made?

The above criticism of FR was made by Pettifor (2014).

Answer. It might seem that under the existing system banks can lend without bothering about whether they have adequate deposits to fund such lending. Or to use a popular phrase "loans precede deposits". That apparent merit in the existing system is in fact entirely illusory, and for the following reasons.

Assume to start with that the economy is at capacity / NAIRU (that assumption is relaxed a few paragraphs hence). If commercial banks create money out of thin air and lend it out, that money must end up in the accounts of various depositors. Now if the latter are not willing to leave the money there for an extended period, i.e. if they are not savers, they will try to spend away their excess stock of money which will raise demand. But that is not permissible if the economy is at capacity. So the central bank will probably raise interest rates, which will cut lending. The net effect, approximately, is "no additional lending".

Alternatively if the central bank does not raise rates, then inflation will ensue, which will cut the value of existing loans in REAL TERMS. So again: "little or no additional lending".

To put all that another way, the fact that loans precede deposits does not mean that lenders can do without depositor / savers. Apples have to be grown before they are eaten. But that does not mean apple growers can do without apple eaters.

As to where the economy IS NOT at capacity, then having commercial banks create money and lend it out would be beneficial. Unfortunately it is very questionable as to whether that actually occurs. That is, as Keynes pointed out, economies can get stuck in high unemployment equilibria, and commercial banks will probably not come to the rescue.

Put another way, commercial bank loan / money creation is pro-cyclical: banks create and lend out money like there is no tomorrow in a boom, exactly when we do not want them to. Then come a recession, their lending / money creation slows down or stops, again, exactly what is not required.

Conclusion. In effect, banks have to find savers before they can lend UNDER THE EXISTING SYSTEM. Thus the fact of having to do the same under FR is irrelevant.

1.13 The basic flaws in Vickers.

Vickers (2011) was roughly speaking the UK equivalent to Dodd-Frank in the US. And the basic remedy for bank problems proposed by Vickers was similar to Glass-Steagall, namely that the bank industry should be split into a safe / retail section and an investment / casino section.

The Vickers commission did consider FR, or so they claimed. In fact as is shown in 2.36 below, they had no grasp of FR. For example Vickers was unaware of the fact that FR has been backed by three economics Nobel Laureates (Freidman, Miller and Tobin). But for the moment, we will just consider the basic flaws in Vickers's proposals which are as follows.

1. According to Vickers, investment banks should be allowed to fail, while retail ones should not. However, Vickers was of course aware of the chaos caused by the collapse of the large US investment bank, Lehmans. So what was Vickers's answer to that dilemma? Well rather than produce some sort of definitive answer to the latter quandary, Vickers just fudged the question as to whether large investment banks should actually be allowed to fail. That is what you might call a bit of a "self-indictment". That is, if you propose that the solution for a problem is to permit X, but you then fudge the question as to whether X should actually be permitted, that indicates muddled thinking.

In contrast, under FR, it is virtually impossible for banks to fail: if they make unwise loans or investments, the value of their shares decline, but they cannot go insolvent. So FR solves the above awkward question which Vickers fudged.

Incidentally it now seems that Lehmans's assets actually exceeded its liabilities all along. In short, the collapse of Lehmans was caused by the risks that the existing banking system allowed it to run. In contrast, under FR, Lehmans would not have collapsed. Indeed, under FR when Lehmans's problems were at their worst, its shares would not even have declined to the extent that shareholders are in it for the long run. And as long as shareholders know that assets of the entity in which they hold shares exceed its liabilities, those shareholders will not be too worried.

2. While it might seem easy to distinguish between bank activities that ought to be in the investment / casino section and the retail / safe section, in fact it is not easy. For example Vickers could not decide which half to place standard banking services for large UK corporations in (Vickers, p.12). And standard banking services for large corporations is a significant chunk of the banking industry!

Now if you postulate that the bank industry (or anything else) falls naturally into two halves, and it then turns out that there are significant shades of grey between the two halves, that seriously calls into question the very idea that the two halves are "natural" in any way. In contrast, under FR, there is a much clearer distinction between the two halves: 1, a totally safe method of lodging money, and 2, a method of lodging money which involves the slightest bit of a risk.

Indeed, the above "large corporation" was far from the only important question that Vickers failed to answer. Kotlikoff (2012, p.60) lists a whole selection of other details which Vickers failed to work out and which they "left to the regulators" to decide.

The latter failure by Vickers to sort out details reinforces a point made earlier, namely that FR has all the beauty of E-MC^2: it is simple and effective. Science attaches importance to simple laws or equations which seem to explain a lot. That is, science is skeptical of complexity.

3. The idea that retail banks are totally safe is clearly not true. A large proportion of, if not the majority of retail banking, consists of loans to mortgagors. And it is clear from those "No Income No Job or Assets" mortgages in the US, that loans to mortgages can go astray or involve excessive risk. And as to the UK, Northern Rock's loans were almost exclusively to mortgagors, yet Northern Rock failed.

In short, the simple fact of separating banking into a safe / retail section and an investment / casino section does not make the first half safe. The conclusion has to be that the BASIC IDEA behind the Vickers proposals is a mess. Of course that Vickers or "Glass-Steagall" type idea can be made to work given a HUGE NUMBER of associated or complementary rules and regulations. But that is not the point. The important point is that FR is simplicity itself. In contrast, Vickers is "complexity itself", which is exactly what the smart lawyers working for banks want. To illustrate, under FR, all the state really needs to check up on is first whether banks have at least as much by way of base money at the central bank and/or government debt as the total amount placed in safe accounts at the bank by depositors. Second, the state or auditors need to check that banks when they claim to be investing money in specific assets (e.g. safe mortgages, the chemical industry or whatever) ACTUALLY invest in those assets. However those sort of checks on EXISTING mutual funds (unit trusts in the UK) do not seem to absorb a huge amount of taxpayers' money, or auditors time, thus there is no reason to suppose the equivalent checks in the case of FR would cost much.

Certainly Merton Miller thought FR would be simple to administer. The last sentence of his paper (Miller (1995)) reads, "Think how much national economic welfare could rise under Fisher's narrow banking scheme when thousands of no longer needed bank regulators (and hundreds of academic banking economists) find themselves forced at last to seek more socially productive lines of economic activity."

1.14 Kotlikoff versus Dyson and Werner.

Dyson (2012) and Werner (2011) advocate an FR system under which lending entities / banks can fail. In contrast, Kotlikoff advocates a system where they cannot. This section compares the two systems and concludes in favor of Kotlikoff.

First, Dyson's system is THE SAME as Kotlikoff / Friedman in that those who want a sum of money to be totally safe have it lodged or invested in a way that is totally safe: i.e. they put it into an entity or account where relevant sums are simply lodged at the central bank (and perhaps also invested in short term government debt).

Also under both systems, those who want their money loaned on or invested have a choice as to what is done with their money.

However, the basic difference between the two systems is

thus. Under Kotlikoffs system, lending entities are funded just by shareholders, thus they cannot fail. In contrast, Dyson and Werner's system promises stakeholders in lending accounts or entities $X back for every $X they invest: which is similar to the EXISTING banking system. And that inevitably means failure is possible. That is, when enough unwise loans are made, the admission has to be made at some point that the game is up, that is, those running the lending entity have to admit that they have failed, and that point the entity is would up, and investors get less than 100 cents in the dollar.

Now the obvious problem with the Dyson / Werner system is that in the event of poor loans being made and the lending entity being wound up, investors end up getting much the same as had the same poor loans been made under the Kotlikoff system! To illustrate, if at some point in time there are only say $0.8 of assets to back every $1 put in by investors / stakeholders, then under Kotlikoff's system, investors would find their stakes were worth about $0.8. In contrast, under Dyson and Werner's system, the bank or mutual fund is wound up and stakeholders get about 80 cents in the dollar. I.e. the basic difference is that when poor loans are made under the Kotlikoff system, the lending entity soldiers on, while under the Dyson / Werner system it is closed down – and for no very good reason.

Or rather Dyson (2012, p.184) does produce some reasons, but they are flawed. He says:

"Investment accounts will be risk-bearing: If some borrowers fail to repay their loans, then the loss will be split between the bank and the holder of the Investment Account. This

sharing of risk will ensure that incentives are aligned correctly, as problems would arise if all the risk fell on either the bank or the investor. For example, placing all the risk on the account holder will incentivise the bank to make the investments that have the highest risk and highest return possible, as the customer would take all the downside of bad investment decisions."

Now there are four problems with that passage, as follows.

1. What does a "bank" consist of under FR? Under FR, the lending entities that replace the lending activities of existing banks scarcely hold any assets. To illustrate, if all sums deposited at a so called "bank" are invested in mutual funds (a la Kotlikoff), what assets does the bank itself have? The answer is "virtually none". Put another way, so called banks under FR become mutual fund administrators (or "fund managers" to quote Coppola (2014)): they become entities that hold few assets. It is thus hard to see how such an "assetless" entity can bear any significant losses.

2. The conflict. The above passage of Dyson's conflicts with the paragraph at the bottom of the same page which says investors (as pointed out above) have a choice as to what is done with their money, and that the categories of assets that investors can go for will be set by government. As Dyson puts it, "The broad categories of investment will need to be set by the authorities".

So, assuming banks obey the law and only put money into say relatively safe mortgages where that's what investors want, then they are not ipso facto being "incentivised to make the investments that have the highest risk and highest return possible..".

3. Existing mutual funds / unit trusts. In fact with EXISTING UNIT TRUSTS (a system where it's essentially those who buy units who carry all losses and profits) there doesn't seem to be a need for government to interfere to any great extent: that is, existing unit trusts which declare they will invest in say German and French government debt or the chemical industry DO JUST THAT: invest in German and French government debt or the chemical industry. I.e. they don't try to allocate money in some sort of underhand way to riskier investments.

The only slight reservation to the latter point is that managers of existing unit trusts are normally on some sort of bonus dependent on the performance of investments they make, and that arguably constitutes "loss splitting" of the sort advocated by Dyson. And there'd be no harm under Dyson's scheme in banks putting investment managers on some sort of bonus. But bonus schemes are common throughout the economy: that is very roughly half the employees in the country are on some sort of bonus scheme. But any such bonus, both with existing unit trusts and under PM's scheme would be a small proportion of total amounts invested and total profits and losses on those investments. So all in all, the latter "bonus" point is near irrelevant.

4. No incentive to take risks. The REASON WHY existing unit trusts / mutual funds do not take big risks and why the funds set up under FR would not do so either is not hard to fathom. It is as follows.

Under the existing banking system, the temptation to take

excessive risks stems from the knowledge that of the risks go badly wrong, the taxpayer foots the bill. In contrast, with a mutual fund, there is no taxpayer waiting to pick up the pieces when it all goes wrong.

Where banks carry all the risk.

Dyson continues:

"Alternatively, if the bank takes all the risk by promising to repay the customer in full regardless of the performance of the investments, then the account holder would face no downside and would consequently only be motivated by high returns, regardless of the risk taken. This would force banks to compete by offering higher interest rates in order to attract funds, which they would then need to invest in riskier projects in order to make a profit."

Well that scenario is to all intents and purposes what the EXISTING bank system involves! Indeed, the last sentence of the latter quote to the effect that the existing system tempts banks to take excessive risk is spot on. I.e. the latter quote is not, as Dyson implies, a way of running a full reserve system: IT IS THE EXISTING SYSTEM.

Conclusion.

Kotlikoff's system is simpler than Dyson and Werner's and better. That is, the basic idea proposed by most FR advocates (certainly Kotlikoff, Milton Friedman, etc) is correct: lending entities / banks should be funded just by shareholders. That is, there is no case for depositors in the traditional sense of the word funding lending entities / banks. However, as pointed out in 1.4 above, there is scope for argument as to what proportion of those shareholders should be ordinary shareholders as opposed to something more in the nature of preference shareholders or "bailinable" bondholders, two types of beast which are effectively shareholders even if (especially in the case of bailinable bond holders) they are not actually called shareholders.

Section 2: Flawed arguments against FR.

This section deals with the large number of arguments put against FR by so called "professional" economists. About half the arguments are anything but "professional". Indeed, demolishing half these arguments requires no knowledge of economics at all: it simply requires a grasp of logic. For a quick taste of some of the dafter arguments, see Nos 7, 8, 13 and 17 below. Each argument below has a heading, followed by one or more of the following.

1. An explanation of the exact nature of the relevant anti-FR argument.

2. A references to works where the relevant anti-FR argument appears.

3. A paragraph normally starting with the word "Answer" in which is the start of the a rebuttal of the relevant anti FR argument.

2.1   FR limits the availability of credit?

That alleged weakness in FR was put by Van Dixhoorn (2013, p.21), Vickers (2011, para 3.21.) and Kregel (2012). See Kregel's passage starting, "In a narrow banking system..". And Coppola (2012) claims FR involves a "serious restriction on the nature and scope of bank lending".

Answer. FR certainly limits the availability of credit in that it requires those who fund loans and investments to carry the risk involved (as opposed to the existing system where the taxpayer carries much of the ultimate risk). And that means the cost of funding loans and investments will rise a bit. But that rise in the cost of borrowing simply reflects the removal of a subsidy. Other than that, there is no reason for the cost of borrowing to rise.

As to the demand reducing effect of that reduced availability of credit, that is easily dealt with by standard stimulatory measures (the measure favored by some advocates of FR, being to simply create new base money and spend it into the economy and/or cut taxes).

As to any other reasons there might be for Coppola's "serious restriction" she does not tell us what they are. The conclusion is that her use of the word "serious" is pure rhetoric. Indeed, the use of emotive phraseology, unbacked by argument or evidence was also the best that Vickers (2011) could do when considering the effect that FR might have on investment (see section 2.36, paragraph starting "Very high…").

As to her "nature and scope", that implies that some forms of lending are reduced more than others. But again, she gives us no details. The conclusion again is that the words "nature and scope" are just there for effect – rhetoric.

There is however a change of the "nature and scope" type that would presumably occur on implementing to FR. That is that under FR, lenders foot the entire bill when loans go wrong, thus IRRESPONSIBLE loans ought to decline under FR.

While Coppola does have a very good grasp of details about what individual banks around the world are doing, she clearly has not bothered to study FR in detail to judge by her comments on Kotlikoff (2012). She claims Kotlikoff's version of FR "includes its own version of what in the UK is known as the Tote". (That's a horse betting system). She then goes on to criticise a system that involves betting along the lines found in horse racing.

Well if banking a la Kotlikoff really did involve something similar to betting on horses, then Coppola would doubtless have a point. However, Tote type betting or "paramutuel" betting is a system that Kotlikoff advocates for INSURANCE COMPANIES, not for banks, as he explains in section 4 of his book.

And finally, mortgage backed Collateralised Debt Obligations (CDOs) are essentially the same thing as a mutual fund under Kotlikoff's version of FR that specialized in mortgages (or an "investment account" under Positive Money's FR system that specialized in mortgages). And in the US, there is no shortage of demand for CDOs. Of course CDOs have become famous for the dishonest techniques used to sell them in recent years. But that is not an argument against the BASIC PRINCIPLE of non money market mutual funds or CDOs, whether they specialize in mortgages or anything else.

2.2 Central bank money is not debt free?

Van Dixhoorn (2013, p.21) claimed that base money, i.e. central bank produced money is not debt free because all money is form of debt.

Answer. In a minor and near irrelevant sense the above "all money is debt" idea is right: that is, base money or central bank created money is NOMINALLY a debt owed by the central bank to the holder of that money. Indeed British £10 notes and other notes actually state "I promise to pay the bearer on demand the sum of £10".

But of course that "promise" is a farce. That is, anyone trying to get £10 of gold (or anything else) from the Bank of England in exchange for their £10 note, would be told to go away (perhaps assisted by the police). Thus the promise on those £10 notes does not prove that base money is "debt encumbered".

In contrast, for every dollar of money created by commercial banks there is, or so it seems, a dollar of debt (owed by a borrower to a commercial bank). But even that argument is debatable (see 3.1 below).

It could be argued that base money is a debt in the following sense. A characteristic of a debt is that it can be used to nullify and equal and opposite debt. Thus when government suddenly demands $X of tax from you, you can use base money to pay them (in fact it's the only money they will accept). Thus it could be argued that base money BECOMES a debt when you receive a tax demand. But that is not the normal meaning of the word "debt".

2.3   Bank capital is expensive for tax reasons?

Increasing bank capital as occurs under FR would involve a cost in that the tax treatment of equity is more onerous than in the case of deposits. That idea was put in a Brookings Institution paper, Elliot (2013).

Answer. The above argument contains an extremely simple flaw, namely that tax is an ENTIRELY ARTIFICIAL imposition, and should thus be ignored. To illustrate, if government taxed red cars more heavily that blue cars, that would raise the price of red cars. But that would not be evidence that the REAL COST of producing red cars was any more than the cost of blue cars.

2.4   FR means the end of banks?

The above was claimed by Coppola (2014) in an article entitled "Martin Wolf Proposes the End of Banking."

The key paragraph of Coppola's article reads *"But there is a problem. The functions that distinguish "banks" from other financial institutions are credit intermediation (deposit-taking and lending) and maturity transformation (borrowing short, lending long). Once banks no longer do either of these, they cannot be regarded as banks. They are simply shops. Once again, we are faced with the death of commercial banking."*

Answer. The fact of proposing a root and branch reform of something to such an extent that normal definitions of the word "bank" or any other word become obsolete is not an argument against such reform. Indeed Klein (2013) in explaining Kotlikoff's verson of FR entitled his article "The Best Way to Save Banking is to Kill It". So Coppola's point that FR in a sense means an end to banking, is a point that advocates of FR are already aware of!

2.5 Central banks will still have to lend to commercial banks?

To deal with lack of credit, the central bank will allegedly still need to lend to commercial banks under FR: exposing the central banks to risks. Thus FR does not dispose of risks for taxpayers – an idea put by Van Dixhoorn (2013). See paragraph starting "Fourth, we consider…"(p.34).

Answer. Given that under FR it is near impossible for a bank to go insolvent (possibly followed by credit crunches etc), there would certainly be FAR LESS NEED under FR for central banks to lend to commercial banks. As to taking that further and having a TOTAL BAN on central bank loans to commercial banks, there are some not bad arguments for that, and as follows.

The flaw in the above argument about lending to commercial banks when there is a "lack of availability of credit" is that it assumes bureaucrats and/or politicians are better judges of what proportion of GDP should be allocated to borrowing, lending and investment than the free market: a highly questionable assumption. Most advocates of FR believe in simply having the authorities implement enough GENERAL STIMULUS to keep the economy at full employment, while market forces determine what PROPORTION of GDP is allocated to investment. Moreover, increased stimulus (i.e. increased demand) will itself increase lenders' willingness to lend. That is, when it comes to deciding whether to lend to a firm, there is nothing that encourages a firm to borrow and a bank to lend like the knowledge that a firm has a healthy order book. As J.K.Galbraith put it, "firms borrow when they can make money, not because interest rates are low".

As to the above questionable judgment of bureaucrats and politicians, a classic example of the sort of false logic used by bureaucrats and politicians occurred in the recent crisis. Essentially they argued that banks have made large losses, therefor they should be supplied with enough taxpayers' money to enable them to get back to approximately where they were before the crisis.

In any normal industry, the fact that losses are made is taken as an indication that the industry is too large and needs to contract. And as to the fact that if the total amount of lending declines if the banking industry declines which in turn reduces aggregate demand, AD can easily be increased by standard stimulatory measures.

Indeed, according to a former governor of the Bank of England, King (2010), the assets of banks in Britain are now TEN TIMES what they were relative to GDP in the 1960s, a period when economic growth was very respect able compared to the disaster of the last five years or so. And that is additional evidence that shrinking the bank industry would do no great harm.

Having said that central bank bureaucrats and politicians are not good judges of how much lending should take place, they are of course able to see when there is a major credit crunch underway, and lend trillions of dollars to commercial banks. But it does not take a genius to be able to see that: reason is that that come a credit crunch, senior commercial bankers appear at the door of central banks and treasuries in a blind panic, begging for trillions of dollars, else (so they tell politicians) the economy will collapse. For example, Sir Tom McKillop, former head of the Royal Bank of Scotland rang up Alistair Darling (Britain's former finance minister) on 7th October 2008 and told Darling that RBS was about to go bust unless it got a huge dollop of public money (see Darling (2008)). Darling actually ended up lending £60bn to two banks, RBS and HBOS. And that is a staggering sum: it represents £1,000 for every man, woman and child in Britain.

Mortgages.

Having argued that central banks should not lend to commercial banks (i.e. that interest rates should be left to find their own level), it could be argued that in the case of mortgages there are SOCIAL implications involved in large interest rate gyrations. But if that strictly social argument can be substantiated, that is an argument for some sort of mortgage subsidy (perhaps just for first time buyers or the less well off), not an argument for using taxpayers' money to iron out fluctuations in interest rates IN GENERAL.

Moreover, SHORT TERM interest rates fluctuate far more dramatically than long term rates, and there is no way taxpayers should subsidise anyone who is effectively taking a bet on future interest rate movements by funding a house purchase with a SHORT TERM loan. Also, as distinct from interest rate FLUCTUATIONS, much higher interest rates over a longish period do not appear to do any harm: rates in the 1980s were FAR HIGHER than nowadays, yet economic growth then was better than over the last five years during which we have enjoyed the dubious benefit of record low rates (as pointed out in section 1.9 above).

Conclusion. There are no good reasons for central banks to support commercial bank lending given a pronounced drop in willingness to lend by commercial banks. But there COULD BE a SOCIAL argument for supporting SPECIFIC TYPES of mortgagor given such a drop.

2.6   FR stops banks producing money from thin air which can fund investments?

When a private bank grants a loan, it might seem that the relevant money comes out of thin air and that money can be used to fund investments. Thus (so it might seem) people do not really need to save in order to fund investments. That idea was put by Pettifor (2014) and Kregel (2012). See Kregel's passage where he claims that FR would create a system "in which all investment decisions…." See Pettifor's paragraph starting "Unlike commodity money…".

Answer. The idea that we don't need to save in order to fund investments (houses, office blocks, etc) is just too good to be true. And as the old saying goes, if anything seems to be too good to be true, it probably is. To put it more bluntly, the idea that we do not need to save or sacrifice current consumption in order to produce investments is straight out of cloud cuckoo land. As explained in section 1.12 above, banks cannot lend without willing savers.

2.7 Investments under FR might not be viable?

That is an idea put by Kregel (2012). See his passage starting "First, the real investments chosen...."

Answer. The advocates of FR do not claim that investors will be any more competent under FR than under the existing system. Clearly under both systems there are, or will be competent and incompetent investors.

2.8 FR will not reduce pleas by failing industries to be rescued by government?

That idea was put by Kregel (2012). See his passage starting "There would always be a risk..."

Answer. Advocates of FR do not claim that FR is a solution to corruption: in particular, politically well-connected individuals trying to extract taxpayers' money from politicians. You really have to wonder what else Kregel will accuse FR of failing to achieve: stopping AIDS or some other disease?

2.9 The cost of converting to FR will be high?

That "high conversion cost" argument was put by Van Dixhoorn (2013, p.21 and Warner (2014).

Answer. Yes, and the cost of building a ship or airliner can be described as "high". But of course the CRUCIAL question is: what is the LONG TERM cost to benefit ratio?

Assuming a country benefits from FR and continues to benefit for the next century or two, then transition costs are probably near irrelevant compared to the long term benefits. Moreover, as one advocate of FR (Friedman (1960 Ch3)) put it *"There is no technical problem of achieving a transition from our present system to 100% reserves easily, fairly speedily, and without serious repercussions on financial or economic markets"*.

2.10 Central bank committees won't be politically neutral?

The argument there is that FR can involve some committee of economists (and perhaps others) deciding on how much money to create and spend, or deciding on other forms of stimulus, and there is no guarantee such a committee will be independent or politically neutral.

That argument was put by Van Dixhoorn (2013, p.22), Pettifor (2014) and Coppola (2012). See Pettifor's paragraph starting "Wolf's proposal is problematic....".

Answer. There are several answers to the above alleged political neutrality problem, and as follows.

1. As explained above, the large majority of economists and indeed the majority of the population are quite happy with specialist committees taking various decisions, both when it

comes to stimulus and in other areas, like health, education and so on. However, and as was also explained above, if the population particularly wanted POLITICIANS ALONE to take stimulus decisions, that would be perfectly feasible under FR.

2. There is no reason why the above alleged problem should be any worse than with EXISTING committees that determine stimulus. For example there is the Bank of England Monetary Policy Committee which has a HUGE INFLUENCE on stimulus (via interest rate adjustments, quantitative easing, etc). Other countries obviously have similar committees. And those committees most certainly do not interfere with strictly political decisions, like how much the country should spend on health or education, or what proportion of GDP should be taken by public spending.

3. Dyson (2012) and Werner (2011) (and doubtless other advocates of full reserve) are VERY SPECIFIC on the point that the above sort of committee should UNDER NO CIRCUMSTANCES interfere with political decisions. The exact way this is done under Dyson's system is for the "committee" to decide HOW MUCH money should be net spent into the economy over the next few months, while the EXACT WAY that money is spend (or whether the adjustment to net spending comes in the form of adjustments to tax) is left ENTIRELY to politicians and voters.

4. It is odd that those who complain about the alleged lack of political neutrality of Positive Money's Money Creation Committee have been very silent about the lack of political neutrality of similar EXISTING committees like the Bank of England MPC in recent years.

2.11 Administration costs of FR would be high?

The "high administration cost" criticism was made by Van Dixhoorn (2014) and Krugman (2014). See Krugman's paragraph starting "Cochrane's proposal calls for…".

Answer. Obviously the central bank or some other body of bank regulators would have to do a fair amount of auditing of commercial banks to make sure they obey the rules. But such auditing is necessary under the EXISTING SYSTEM. Moreover, compare that with the rules which make up the Dodd-Frank regulations: those stand at 10,000 pages and counting. Compared to Dodd-Frank and Vickers (2011), FR is simplicity itself.

2.12 The cost of current accounts will rise under FR?

That criticism was put by Van Dixhoorn (2013, p.22) and Aziz (2014).

Answer. It is true that under FR, those with transaction / safe / current / checking accounts get little or no interest: i.e. probably less interest than on such accounts under the existing system. However interest under the existing system only comes as a result of being able to have one's money loaned on or invested with the taxpayer carrying the ultimate risk. But the latter is a totally unwarranted "have your cake and eat it" subsidy.

If restaurants had been subsidised for the last century and that subsidy was removed, then (to use Van Dixhoorn's phrase) "losses would be imposed on" those eating at restaurants. But that would not justify continuing to subsidise restaurants.

2.13. FR is dependent on demand injections?

Kregel (2012) made that criticism.

Answer. It would be nice to know how Kregel would describe the trillions of dollars recently used to bail out the bank industry and the large amounts of stimulus needed to rectify the effects of the recent crisis. Kregel uses the phrase "chronically dependent on demand injections" in reference to FR. The phrase would seem more appropriate to the existing banking system, rather than to FR.

Moreover, stimulus costs nothing in real terms: to put it figuratively, printing and spending dollar bills (and/or cutting taxes) costs nothing. Or as Friedman (1960, Ch 3) put it, "It need cost society essentially nothing in real resources to provide the individual with the current services of an additional dollar in cash balances."

2.14 The effect of FR on inflation and unemployment is unclear?

That criticism was put by Van Dixhoorn (2013). As Van Dixhoorn put it: "it would be difficult to predict what the ultimate effects on output and inflation would be..".

Answer. There is NO NEED WHATEVER to predict the

effect on output or inflation because the latter two can be adjusted (just as they are under the existing system) by adjusting stimulus. That of course is done under the existing system by adjusting interest rates, QE, the size of the deficit, etc. In contrast, most advocates of FR advocate a slightly different form of stimulus (which actually amounts to fiscal stimulus plus QE). But that's a minor technical point.

Moreover, under the EXISTING SYSTEM, governments have only the haziest ideas as to what inflation and unemployment will be five years from now: e.g. there might be another credit crunch, or there might not. Thus the above criticism applies to the EXISTING SYSTEM as much as it does to FR.

2.15 FR would drive business to the unregulated sector?

That criticism was made by Krugman (2014): passage starting "If we impose 100% reserve.." and by Diamond (1986) and by Vickers (2011 , 4.36).

Answer. Clearly if government regulates just one part of an industry, that will cause a number of operators to flee to the unregulated sector. Indeed over the last decade there has been a shift of business away from official banks and into the shadow bank sector. But the simple solution to that is to regulate ANY ENTITY above a certain size that amounts to a bank.

As the former head of the UK's Financial Services Authority, Turner (2012) put it: "If it looks like a bank and quacks like a bank, it has got to be subject to bank-like safe-guards."

Indeed, regulating one half of the banking industry but not the other half (the shadow banking industry) makes about as much sense as forcing male drivers to abide by speed limits, but not female drivers, or vice versa.

2.16 The state cannot be trusted with peoples' money?

The idea there is that the so called "safe accounts" set up under FR are not entirely safe, a criticism made by (Van Dixhoorn (2013) section VIII, p.32.

Answer. Clearly governments are not entirely reliable and for two reasons. First, governments may cause excess inflation, which means that sums deposited in safe accounts lose their value, and second, governments have been known to renege on promises to return sums they have borrowed or which have been lodged with them. However, neither of those two points are good criticisms of FR and for the following reasons.

As to inflation, if money lodged at the central bank is losing its value, then money lodged at a private bank will lose value at exactly the same rate.

And as to the point that governments can renege on promises to return monies lodged with them, the sort of government which does that is quite likely to also confiscate monies lodged at private banks.

Moreover, FR is a system suitable for a country with a reasonably responsible government. Obviously where government is near non-existent or chaotic, citizens might well be better off keeping their savings under the mattress and/or in the form of valuables like a rare metal.

And finally, under the existing system, millions of UK citizens seem to be happy to lodge a portion of their money with National Savings and Investments, a state run savings bank. That is, the reality is that a large proportion of the population in Britain or any "non-chaotic" country regard government as being responsible enough to be entrusted with a portion of their wealth.

2.17 Vested interests would oppose FR?

The Economist (2014) claimed that vested interests would oppose FR. Their exact words were: "there would be formidable opposition from vested interests"

Answer. The abolition of slavery was opposed by formidable "vested interests". Do we take it The Economist would have opposed the abolition of slavery? In short, the fact that "vested interests" want X or Y is no argument for X or Y. Indeed, if anything it's an argument AGAINST X or Y.

However, credit where credit is due: The Economist were at least correct to say that FR would be opposed by "vested interests". Although that is not a brilliantly perceptive point in that ANY ATTEMPT to clean up the corrupt cess-pit that is banking will clearly be opposed by "vested interests".

Incidentally Milton Friedman's explanation for the failure to implement FR cited vested interests (Friedman (1960)). As he put it, *"The vested political interests opposing it are too strong, and the citizens who would benefit both as taxpayers and as participants in economic activity are too unaware of its benefits and too disorganised to have any influence."*

2.18 FR will reduce innovation by banks?

That criticism was put by Van Dixhoorn (2013, p.22) and Aziz (2014).

Answer. Under the EXISTING SYSTEM, commercial banks introduced debit and credit cards because those cards are more efficient for many transactions than cash or cheques. Any bank that had ignored those innovations would have lost customers. And exactly the same would apply under FR. That is, under FR, commercial banks would open current / checking / safe accounts for customers. And as to the EXACT WAY in which payments are made, that would be up to individual banks. And competitive forces would induce banks to adopt any sort of new technology (e.g. payment by mobile phones) just as those forces induce them to adopt new technology under the existing system.

2.19 Deposit insurance and lender of last resort solves banking problems?

I.e. there is no need for FR, a claim made by Aziz (2014)).

Answer. As to the existing deposit insurance system, the problems with that were dealt with in section 1.4 above.

As to lender of last resort (a luxury not available to other industries) that is a SUBSIDY of the banking industry. As it explains in the introductory economics text books, subsidies misallocate resources, that is, they reduce GDP (unless some very good social justifications can be found for the subsidies.)

Incidentally, and contrary to common perception, Walter Bagehot did not approve of lender of last resort (Bagehot (1873), final chapter). He regarded it as something that was so ingrained in the system that it would be impossible to remove.

2.20 Lenders will try to turn their liabilities into "near-monies"?

Van Dixhoorn (2013) p.33 put the above "near monies" criticism.

Answer. Obviously some lenders will try to do that. In fact advocates of FR in the 1930s were well aware of that potential problem as are present day advocates of FR, Dyson (2012) in particular.

But dealing with that problem is not difficult. For example it would be easy to require all literature and web sites dealing with non-money market mutual funds under Kotlikoff's FR system to declared in bold type something to the effect that "You are not guaranteed $X back for every $X you invest in this fund." In fact in the UK the law already requires those selling unit trusts and other stock exchange investments to declare something very similar: a sentence to the effect that "the value of these investments can fall as well as rise".

Second, it can be made illegal to draw checks or do plastic card transactions on a stake in a bank which consists nominally of shares. Indeed under the FR system advocated by Dyson (2012) and Werner (2011), checks and plastic card transactions can only be funded by safe accounts.

2.21 Anyone can create money, thus trying to limit money creation is futile?

See Van Dixhoorn (2013) - paragraph starting "The sector will..." p.34).

Answer. The text book definition of the word money is something like "anything widely accepted in payment for goods and services".

Now the liabilities of banks are "widely accepted" because they are SPECIFICALLY DISIGNED to be easily transferrable. In contrast, it is quite untrue to suggest, as Van Dixhoorn does that an ordinary trade credit is a form of money. To illustrate, if firm A delivers goods to firm B worth $X, B is then indebted to A to the tune of $X. And B could issue an IOU in payment. But is that liability (the IOU) likely to be of any use to A for the purposes of "paying money" to some third party? It is unlikely. Thus an ordinary trade credit just isn't money in a large majority of cases.

The latter form of "IOU" money creation was more common

in the 1700s and 1800s: the IOUs took the form of bills of exchange. But those are rare nowadays.

But that is not to say that after implementing FR there would be a total absence of types of money other than what the average household or firm regards as money, or other than what might be called "official" money. In particular, in the world's financial centres various types of debt serve the purpose of money: e.g. short term government debt. However for the large majority of households and the large majority of firms, particularly small and medium size ones, there is only one form of money and that is central bank created money and money created by well-known commercial banks which trades at par with central bank money.

Local currencies. Another form of money or quasi-money that could perfectly well be left in place on implementing FR is local currencies. Though it is actually debatable as to how far local currencies constitute money and for the following reason.

Money is defined in economics dictionaries (as pointed out above) as something like: "anything widely accepted in payment for goods and services". Now local currencies are not "accepted" outside particular localities. Thus they do not fulfil the "widely accepted" criterion. Indeed, they are probably not even accepted for the majority of transactions WITHIN the relevant areas.

2.22 Advocates of FR are concerned just with retail banking?

That was claimed by Van Dixhoorn (2013, paragraph starting "Third the critics have.." p.34 and Krugman (2014).

Answer. The above criticism is just nonsense. If those making that criticism bothered to read the literature, they would find that advocates of FR apply the same rules to investment banks as to retail banks. To repeat: that is one of the beauties of FR – it solves several bank related problems with a few simple rules.

2.23 The government and/or central bank will not be better than the market at regulating the amount of money?

That criticism was put by Warner (2014) passage starting "..it takes quite a leap to think..". Coppola (2012) makes the same claim.

Answer. At the time of writing, we have just been thru a crisis caused by a catastrophic failure of private banks to regulate the amount of money / loans in a stable manner. Thus the above alleged weakness in FR flies in the face of reality.

Moreover, most of those who make the above criticism seem quite happy for government and central bank to regulate aggregate demand, and ironically, one way that the authorities do that (as already pointed out) is fiscal stimulus plus QE, which amounts to exactly the form of stimulus advocated by most supporters of FR! In short, Warner contradicts himself.

As to Coppola, she tries to substantiate her claim that the committee that determined stimulus under FR would not ACCURATELY estimate the amount of stimulus correctly by referring to an EXISTING and similar committee that seems to be not too good at forecasting. As she puts it "The Office of Budget Responsibility's October evaluation report admitted that they got their growth forecasts wrong by a full 5 percentage points."

Now it's a bit odd to criticise a PROPOSED system by pointing to a defect in the EXISTING system! If the existing system is so defective, that rather suggests something else might be better. At the very least, all Coppola's above criticism amounts to is saying that committees of economists are far from perfect when it comes to forecasting. No doubt they are, and no doubt members of those committees would be first to admit to their imperfections. But that's not an argument for or against a different type of committee.

2.24 It wasn't just banks that failed in 2008: also households became over-indebted?

That criticism was put by Krugman (2014). See his paragraph starting "Third....".

Answer. First, who were those households indebted to? It was banks to some extent! If lending entities / banks become more responsible under FR because they know there is no taxpayer to pay for the irresponsibility when it goes wrong, then that would reduce the "over-indebted" problem to which Krugman refers.

Second, of course it was not JUST BANKS that households were indebted to: that is banks sold on mortgages to non-bank entities. Thus households were effectively in debt to the latter entities, not to banks. And clearly FR does not cut irrational exuberance in that area. But nor does it stop stock exchange irrational exuberance. FR, to repeat, does not solve every conceivable economic problem.

Third, Krugman makes much of the fact that banks recovered relatively quickly from the crisis, in contrast to which indebted households took much longer to recover (see Krugamn's chart). Well you bet banks recovered quickly: they were the lucky recipients of trillions of dollars of public money: loans at favorable rates of interest and so on! It is precisely the latter sort of subsidy or distortion that is disposed of under FR.

2.25 Creation of liquidity / money is prevented?

See Diamond (1986).

Answer. True, but that is half the object of the exercise. That is, advocates of FR claim that just the central bank should create money, while commercial banks continue to act as intermediaries between borrowers and lenders much as they do at present (with the exception that lenders carry all losses when poor loans are made rather than the taxpayer carrying some of those losses as occurs at present).

As to the arguments against private money creation were set out in section 1.5 above.

Finally, one has to wonder how much of a grip on reality Diamond has given that the word "subsidy" does not appear in his paper. One of the main merits of full reserve is that it disposes of bank subsidies. Plus it is widely agreed even by those who DO NOT support FR, that the TBTF and other bank subsidies should be disposed of. In short, Diamond, either by error or by design, keeps very quiet about a major defect in the banking system he advocates.

2.26 Funding via commercial paper would be more difficult under FR?

See Diamond (1986).

Answer. Loans based on commercial paper are just one form of loan. The important question is to work out what is the best banking / lending / borrowing system for ALL TYPES of lender and borrower.

2.27 FR is nearly the same as monetarism?

See Pettifor (2014).

Answer. The basic flaw in the above criticism of FR is that the criticism is hopelessly vague, and for the following reasons.

Monetarism is at its simplest just the idea that the QUANTITY of money is of some relevance: that the quantity of money has some sort of effect. And it is pretty obvious that the quantity of money must have SOME SORT OF effect. About 95% of economists are agreed on the latter very simple and obvious point.

Milton Friedman was famous of course for taking that to an extreme: claiming that economies can be regulated JUST BY adjusting the quantity of money. In fact he went even further and claimed that that quantity should be expanded by the same small amount year in year out regardless of whether the economy was booming or in a recession.

Thus the simple statement that "FR is similar to monetarism" is virtually meaningless: is that statement simply a claim that FR includes the banal idea that the quantity of money has some sort of effect? Or is, at the other extreme, to claim that FR equals Friedman's extreme version of the latter banal point?

Moreover, advocates of FR (like the majority of economists probably) also claim that THE PROCESS OF spending extra money created into the economy also has an effect. I.e. they claim fiscal boost has an effect. Thus even if the quantity of money has virtually no effect, that does not greatly dent or destroy the "create new money and spend it or cut taxes" idea put by some advocates of FR, and indeed others who do not support FR.

2.28 No demand for safe or warehouse banks?

Numerous critics of FR claim there has been no demand throughout history for banks which simply lodge money without lending it on and thus earning depositors some interest. Thus there would be no demand for the safe accounts under FR. For example White (2003) and Van Dixhoorn (2013) make that criticism.

Answer. First, that contradicts the equally common claim by opponents of FR that there'd be a **stampede for** safe accounts. See section 2.29 just below.

Second, the claim flies in the face of the facts. That is, most people want to spread their risks: e.g. store some of their wealth (liquid and illiquid) in very safe forms, while doing something more daring or risky with another portion of their wealth. And in fact there are numerous very safe types of bank or quasi-bank: there is National Savings and Investments in the UK and money market mutual funds in the US which invest in nothing more risky than base money and/or short term government debt.

It is true that the latter don't pay a ZERO rate of interest, but the rate paid is very low, reflecting the safe nature of investments. Thus there would presumably be a finite demand for an account which involved even greater safety and paid an even lower rate.

Moreover, to the extent that there IS A LIMITED demand for warehouse banking since WWII, that is hardly surprising. Reason is that taxpayer funded backing for conventional banks enables ordinary depositors to enjoy total safety while getting interest. Why go for an account that pays no interest when you can get interest gratis the taxpayer?

2.29 FR would cause a stampede to safe accounts?

The above was claimed by Dowd (2014).

Answer. First, that contradicts the claim made by several opponents of FR, namely that there'd be no demand for safe accounts - see section 2.28 just above. Second, a large or small degree of flight to safety is nothing to get excited about. If the extent of flight is small, that is nice in that the cost of funding banks will rise by a relatively small amount. But if the degree of flight is relatively large, that just demonstrates the extent to which bank funding is currently supported by taxpayer funded guarantees of safety for depositors. And those guarantees amount to a subsidy of banks which distorts markets and reduces GDP.

2.30 FR would raise the cost of funding banks?

That is, it might seem that the cost of funding banks rises because shareholders demand a bigger return on their investment than depositors. Thus if the proportion of bank funding that comes from shares as opposed to deposits is increased then the cost of funding banks would seem to rise.

Answer. The flaw in the above argument was set out by Franco Modigliani and Merton Miller, as explained in more detail in section 1.4 above. Just to summarise though, as they explained, the risks involved in running a bank which performs a given set of activities is a GIVEN. Thus the price charged by those covering that risk is also a given. Thus increasing the proportion of bank funding that comes from shares rather than deposits and similar has no effect on the total charge that shareholders make for covering the risk.

But FR does raise the cost of funding banks in that bank subsidies are removed. However removing subsidies ought to INCREASE GDP not REDUCE it.

2.31 Fractional reserve is not fraudulent?

White (2003) claimed that fractional reserve (i.e. the existing banking system is not fraudulent. (Incidentally the phrase "fractional reserve" is a bit of a misnomer as is "full reserve" (as explained above) but it is a phrase that has established itself.)

Answer. The first problem there is that White in the latter work doesn't say what the alleged fraud actually is. Instead, he refers on his first page to about ten books and articles which apparently set out the fraud. It is thus impossible to know what fraud or alleged fraud White refers to.

Second, given the number of works he cites that apparently set out the fraud, it's unlikely those works all agree with each other. Indeed, there are several popular "fraud" charges made against fractional reserve which are clearly invalid.

However, White's central point is that for fraud to exist, someone must be duped, and the large majority of bank customers do not regard themselves as having being duped.

The flaw in that argument is that there are all degrees of "duping" from slight misrepresentation to serious and carefully thought out fraud. And the extent of misrepresentation doubtless varies depending on the fraud involved.

However, as a second best, let us consider White's arguments as they relate a "fraud" charge against fractional reserve which does have some substance, and which is as follows.

A fractional reserve bank promises to return to depositors and bondholders the exact sum deposited (maybe plus interest and maybe less bank charges). But of course the flaw or fraud there is that the money is loaned on or invested by the bank and that involves the risk that the loans or investments go bad. And sure as night follows day, once every twenty or thirty years the loans do go wrong, and one or more large banks can't repay all the money they owe depositors. And as to small banks in the US, they go bust at the rate of about one a week.

So how much fraud or misrepresentation takes place there? Well commercial banks certainly do not advertising the fact that there is a one in twenty chance that depositors and similar bank creditors will lose their money! Quite the reverse: their publicity normally stresses the safety of the relevant bank. So there is certainly AN ELEMENT of fraud there.

Of course the contract governing an account at a typical bank, the small print in particular, may say something different. But that's near irrelevant. The typical bank customer does not read the small print - and probably wouldn't understand it if they did. It is thus indisputable that banks are guilty of a certain amount of misrepresentation or to put it more strongly – "fraud" and "duping".

The actual degree of fraud perpetrated by fractional reserve banks actually depends on their capital ratios. To illustrate, capital ratios of about 3% were common before the recent crisis. In that scenario, a bank effectively declares that it will not go technically or actually insolvent because there is a minimal chance of its assets falling in value by more than about 3%, a claim which is clearly absurd and blatantly fraudulent.

However, the higher the capital ratio, the less the fraud until one reaches the 100% ratio. But that is FR pure and simple and totally fraud free!

Bonds issued by non-bank corporations.

A weakness in the latter argument might seem to be that if a promise by a bank to return £X to its creditors is fraudulent, then so too are bonds issued by non-bank corporations. The answer to that is that strictly speaking all bonds of that type are fraudulent, however those purchasing such bonds are not typical households who seriously believe the "promise to return": they are sophisticated investors who know perfectly well that if the relevant corporation fails badly, they will lose out. Thus those investors are not duped. Moreover, bonds in non-bank corporations are never counted as a form of money. And the crisis inducing effect of £Y of the nation's money disappearing is much worse than bond-holders discovering they've lost £Y.

2.32 FR will not stop boom and bust?

Turner (2010, p.45-6) made the above criticism. As he put it in relation to Kotlikoff's non money market mutual funds:

"...investors would be likely in the upswing to consider their investments as safe as bank deposits. Investments in loan funds would therefore be likely to grow in a pro-cyclical fashion when valuations were on an upswing and then to run when valuations and confidence fell, creating credit booms and busts potentially as severe as in past bank-based crises."

Answer. The advocates of FR do not claim that FR will totally eliminate all instabilities. Nothing will ever totally eliminate bouts of irrational exuberance or the opposite.

However, there is a fundamental difference between FR and the existing system. Under FR, all lenders essentially become shareholders, and it is virtually impossible for banks / lending entities under FR to go insolvent. And as two former central bank governors, King (2010) and Greenspan (2014) pointed out, a fall in share values causes minimal disturbance as compared to banks going insolvent. As King put it,

"...we saw in 1987 and again in the early 2000s, that a sharp fall in equity values did not cause the same damage as did the banking crisis. Equity markets provide a natural safety valve, and when they suffer sharp falls, economic policy can respond. But when the banking system failed in September 2008, not even massive injections of both liquidity and capital by the state could prevent a devastating collapse of confidence and output around the world."

Or as Greenspan put it:

"All bubbles expand, and they all collapse. But how they are financed is critical. The dot-com boom [of 1994 to 2000] produced a huge financial collapse with almost no evidence of economic impact."

Of course, a decline in large swathes of stock market shares is not the same thing as a decline just in shares in lending entities. Nevertheless, there is a big difference between, first, a system that results in lending entities closing their doors given problems, and two, a system that simply results in shares in such entities declining. The first scenario is clearly the more serious.

2.33 Bank shareholders will demand a high return to reflect their uncertainty about what a bank actually does?

I.e. bank management knows more about its bank that shareholders or potential shareholders, thus the latter will want insurance against possibly being misinformed by bank management, thus equity is an inherently expensive way of funding banks, a claim made by Elliot (2013).

Answer. Depositors and bond-holders who fund banks suffer from EXACTLY THE SAME asymmetric information problem. Thus Elliot's point is not an argument for reducing or increasing capital ratios.

2.34 FR reduces commercial bank flexibility?

The idea that under FR, individual banks are constrained by the need to find savers before they can lend was shown to be flawed in section 1.12 above.

As distinct from INDIVIDUAL banks, there is the possibility that FR constrains the ability of the commercia bank system AS A WHOLE to expand the aggregate amount loaned. Well perhaps FR does have that effect, but that's not entrely unwelcomed given that fact that in the UK, commercial bank loans / money expanded at a rapid rate in the three years or so just prior to the crises. And that resulted in a boom followed by a bust.

Then, as always happens in busts, commercial banks did exactly what we do not want them to do, i.e. put the whole process into reverse: they called in loans, etc. In short, the commercial bank system EXACERBATES the boom bust cycle.

To summarise, when there is a faster than usual expansion in the amount of commercial bank lending, that's probably a sign of a boom or bubble. In contrast, if the money supply is under the control of the central bank, it can expand the money supply in a way desiged to be in the best interests of the country as a whole: i.e. in accordance with what inflation and unemployment are doing.

Moreover, opponents of FR (i.e. defenders of the existing banking system) are perfectly happy for central banks and governments to try and control the boom / bust cycle via interest rate adjustments, quantitative easing and so on, and the latter necessarily involves influencing the amount of commercial bank lending. Those opponents of FR thus need to explain why they object so much to commercial bank lending being controlled in a slightly different way, as occurs under FR.

2.35 FR would not stop bank runs?

I.e. given suspicions about a lending entity, its shares might be dumped in the same way as depositors withdraw their money en masse from a traditional bank about which there are suspicions.

Answer. No. There is an important difference between a traditional bank and an entity funded just by shares. In the case of the former, a run can and does quickly lead to insolvency. In the case of the latter, insolvency is virtually impossible. As Cochrane (2013) put it, "the financial system needs to be reformed so that it is not prone to runs."

2.36 Vickers's flawed criticisms of FR.

The BASIC flaws in the ideas put by Vickers (2011) were set out in Section 1.13 above. In contrast, this section runs through Vickers's criticisms of FR (see Vickers's paragraphs 3.20 to 3.24).

Section 3.20.

This starts:

"Proponents of a different kind of structural reform known as 'narrow banking' (Kay (2009)) argue that the function of taking deposits and providing payments services to individuals and SMEs is so critical to the economy that it should not be combined with risky assets. Under a strict form of narrow banking the only assets allowed to be held against such deposits would be safe, liquid assets."

There two problems with that passage, as follows.

First, the passage refers to "narrow" banking which amounts to the same thing as the safe accounts offered by FR. But a few paragraphs later (3.22) Vickers refers to "limited purpose banking" which they say *"offers an alternative solution, under which the role of financial intermediaries is to bring together savers and borrowers but risk is eliminated from the intermediary because it does not hold the loan on its books. All of the risk of the loan is passed onto the investors…"*.

But "limited purpose banking" comes to the same thing as the lending/investing half of the bank industry under FR. Moreover, if the law says that those wanting total safety must put their money into an account where funds are not loaned on, then it follows that lending must be and will be done by entities of the "lending/investing" type (funded by shareholders). Thus to describe limited purpose banking as an "alternative solution" as Vickers does, indicates a failure to understand the basic issue here.

That is, the reality is that narrow banking and limited purpose banking are necessarily and logically all part of the same system, which is commonly referred to as "full reserve" or "100% reserve" banking.

Second, and regarding Vickers's reference to Kay (2009), John Kay actually contradicts himself. He does initially say "The model of narrow banking is one in which all retail deposits are secured on safe assets." But then on his p.52 he says "Narrow banks might engage in consumer lending, lend on mortgage, and lend to businesses, but would not enjoy a monopoly of these functions."

That's an absolutely fundamental self-contradiction. So this looks like a case of the blind leading the blind. But never mind: let's run with Kay's first or initial ideas as to what narrow banking consists of (as per Vickers). Vickers continues:

"Since lending to the private sector necessarily involves risk, such banks would not be able to use the funding from deposits to make loans to individuals and SMEs. Should ring-fenced banks be allowed to make such loans? If ring-fenced banks were not able to perform their core economic function of intermediating between deposits and loans, the economic costs would be very high."

"Very high"? Where do they get that from? Well here's a clue. On the subject of "very high", Vickers's so called "Interim Report" said something very similar to their "Final Report". The interim report actually said *"Like narrow banking, a complete move from fractional to full reserve banking would drastically curtail the lending capacity of the UK banking system, reducing the amount of credit available to households and businesses and destroying intermediation synergies."*

But according to Dyson (2012, p.267), *"In response to*

requests, the commission would not clarify what they meant by "drastic"".

In short, and as far as those phrases "very high" and "drastic" go, it very much looks as though Vickers is making it up as it goes along.

But never mind. It's not too difficult to come up with some more intelligent ideas here than Vickers managed as regards the effect of full reserve banking on *"...the amount of credit available to households and businesses".*

Under full reserve, those funding businesses and mortgages have to bear the full cost of what they do, as distinct from the existing system under which taxpayers bear the ultimate risk involved in that funding or lending. And that's the main difference between the existing system and full reserve.

Thus full reserve DOES INVOLVE increased costs for borrowers, BUT ONLY TO THE EXTENT of removing the above taxpayer funded subsidy. Moreover, Vickers's two reports (interim and final) just like Dodd-Frank clearly state that subsidies are undesirable.

So Vickers advocates the removal of bank subsidies at the same time as objecting to a system which actually removes those subsidies! It very much looks as though Vickers is in check mate there.

The rest of section 3.21.

The rest of this section does not add much to the above points, though the final two sentences of this section are worth examining. The first says:

"Either way, narrow banking would mean that ring-fenced banks could not be a source of stable credit supply during times of stress".

Now there is a definitial problem there, namely that Vickers proposes splitting the bank industry into two halves one way, and full reserve proposes splitting it another. Thus using the phrase "ringfence" when considering full reserve is not entirely logical. However, let's assume that "ring-fenced banks" means banks which concentrate on the retail and small firm sectors (and doubtless such banks or lending entities would arise under FR).

The advocates of FR and Vickers are agreed that it is important for households and small firms to be able to pay each other given problems with the investment or casino section of the banking system. But full reserve achieves that by making TOTALLY safe accounts available. In contrast, Vickers's supposedly safe "ring fenced" sector of the banking industry is NOT TOTALLY SAFE because it lends out money in a less than 100% safe fashion. Thus Vickers's claim just above that full reserve's equivalent of ring fenced banks "could not be a source of stable credit supply during times of stress" is very questionable if not pure nonsense: FR's safe accounts are SAFER THAN Vickers's equivalent.

As to why retail lending entities under FR would not be a "source of stable credit" Vickers does not explain. Certainly there is no reason to suppose there'd be any wild gyrations in the total amount that investor / depositors want to have loaned on to mortgagors, businesses and so on.

Moreover, the EXISTING BANKING SYSTEM is a hundred

miles from offering a "stable source of credit" to potential borrowers. As explained above, under the existing system the amount of bank credit varies greatly depending on whether the economy is in boom or bust mode. And also as explained above, booms and busts ought to less severe under FR. So to that extent, the amount of credit available under FR ought to be MORE STABLE than under the existing system.

The last sentence of 3.21.

In the last sentence of this section Vickers says:

"Instead, the supply of credit would move entirely to a less regulated sector."

The answer to that point was spelled out in section 2.15 above, the answer being briefly that it is nonsense to have a regulated and non-regulated banking sector. That is ANY ENTITY involved in lending should abide by the same rules (regardless, incidentally, of whether FR is implemented or not).

Section 3.22.

This section starts:

"Limited purpose banking offers an alternative solution, under which the role of financial intermediaries is to bring together savers and borrowers but risk is eliminated from the intermediary because it does not hold the loan on its books. All of the risk of the loan is passed onto the investors in the intermediary (or fund), so that effectively all debt is

securitised.

However, limited purpose banking would severely constrain two key functions of the financial system. First, it would constrain banks' ability to produce liquidity through the creation of liabilities (deposits) with shorter maturities than their assets. The existence of such deposits allows households and firms to settle payments easily."

Well the answer to that "constrain" point was spelled out in section 1.5 above. Briefly the answer is that the arguments for having commercial banks create a form of money just do not stand inspection.

As for the idea that "existence of such deposits allows households and firms to settle payments easily", what's the relevance of that point? Vickers seems to suggest that under FR "households and firms" wouldn't have a method of "settling payments easily" which is of course nonsense: under FT, "households and firms" have current or checking accounts just as under the existing system.

Monitoring borrowers.

Vickers continues:

"Second, banks would no longer be incentivised to monitor their borrowers, and it would be more difficult to modify loan agreements. These activities help to maximise the economic value of bank loans."

"No longer incentivised to monitor"? What on Earth is

Vickers on about? It's under the EXISTING SYSTEM that there is a lack of "incentive to monitor" because lenders know that taxpayers stand behind them!! And Vickers fails to dispose of that taxpayer backing or subsidy for the bank industry!

As to the idea that it would be "difficult to modify loan agreements", the logic there will probably elude most readers, if not all of them. Under full reserve, lenders and borrowers are free to set up loan agreements in any way they want, as long as it is not illegal. If lenders want to insist that borrowers drink whiskey rather than gin (to take a silly example), contracting parties are entirely free under the law of most countries to include that condition in loan agreements under both the existing system and under full reserve. And if they want to "modify" the amount of whisky drinking involved in the loan, that's entirely up to the contracting parties. Same goes for "modifying loan agreements".

Section 3.23.

This section starts with a reference to Vickers's "ring fence" proposal: that's the idea that risky or investment banking be separated from retail banking.

"The ring-fence proposal shares the recognition that continuous provision of deposit taking services is important to the economy, but not the conclusion that the providers of such services must therefore be made virtually riskless. The role banks play in intermediation is an important one, and lending necessarily involves risk. So some risk of failure should be tolerated but it must be possible for the authorities to ensure continuous provision of vital services without

taxpayer support for the creditors of a failed provider."

Pray how does Vickers propose combining a "risk of failure" with an absence of "taxpayer support of the creditors of a failed provider"? That is a straight self-contradiction. That is, in the event of a "provider failing", Vickers does not want creditors (especially depositors) to foot the bill, nor does Vickers want taxpayers to foot the bill.

SO WHO DOES FOOT THE BILL? Vickers doesn't tell us!

Vickers continues:

"Equally, the importance of intermediation means that it should not be combined with other risky activities which are not an inherent part of intermediation."

But Vickers just said in the previous sentence that intermediators should be involved in "some risk of failure". To put it mildly, there is some muddled thinking here.

Section 3.24.

This starts:

"The debate about narrow banking provides two important insights into the appropriate design of a retail ring-fence:

• services which are not integral to the direct intermediation of funds or the provision of payments services should not be provided by ring-fenced banks...."

Now wait a moment. Investment banks do carry out "intermediation"!

The conclusion has to be that the BASIC IDEA behind the Vickers proposals is a mess. Of course it can be made to work given a HUGE NUMBER of associated or complementary rules and regulations. But that is not the point. The important point is that FR is simplicity itself. In contrast, Vickers is "complexity itself", which is exactly what the smart lawyers working for banks want.

2.37 Regulating loans is better than FR?

I.e. an obvious way to make banks safer is to impose more stringent regulations on lenders for example insisting on minimum equity stakes for mortgagors (i.e. insisting on maximum loan to value ratios for mortgagors). And that is an alternative, if not a better option than FR.

Answer. The first problem there is that that is relatively easy to do in the case of mortgages, but not in the case of loans to businesses. For example some bank managers, quite rightly, lend to particular businesses because they know the relevant business proprietors and know the latter to be competent. Setting up rules and regulations to cater for those elusive characteristics of entrepreneurs is impossible.

Second, even if it were possible to forbid the making of risky loans, it is hard to see the case for doing so where lender and borrower now what they are doing, and assuming there are no harmful systemic consequences when a significant proportion of those loans go wrong. And the latter is exactly what FR achieves because when a significant number of loans go wrong, lending entities do not become insolvent: all that happens is that shares in lending entities decline in value.

Moreover, under FR, those who fund loans are free to have their money loaned on in whatever way they want: if they really want to fund NINJA mortgages, they are free to do so. Free markets and capitalism are all about taking risks: sometimes small risks and sometimes big risks. If big risks had been banned over the last three hundred years, the industrial revolution would never have taken place.

In short, regulating loans achieves stability by cutting down on flexibility. In contrast, under FR, stability is achieved without reducing flexibility.

2.38 FR doesn't insure against liquidity shocks?

Bossone (2002) claimed: "An important strand of research, following Diamond and Dybvig (1983), stress the role of banks as insurers against liquidity shocks."

Answer. Some readers may fall about laughing at that claim, reason being that it was the banking system ITSELF which around 2005 was the MAJOR CAUSE OF a "liquidity shock". It was TAXPAYERS who provided TRILLIONS OF DOLLARS of "insurance money" to deal with the "liquidity shock".

In fact Bossone seems to be very much in awe of the responsible and prudent behaviour of banks when he claims "This crucial link between liquidity and production is explicitly recognized in Diamond and Rajan (1998, 1999), where banks are regarded as superior devices to tie human capital with real (illiquid) assets, and where the sequential service constraint ordering the way in which banks service withdrawal demands (up to when they become illiquid) work as an incentive for bankers to behave prudently."

So bankers behave "prudently" under the existing system do they? The reality is that they were responsible for the worst crash since 1929. Moreover, to judge by the multi billion dollar fines paid by banks around 2013-14 for various crimes and misdeeds, it would be reasonable to say that banks are the biggest criminal organisations in the Western world. In short, the word "prudent" in this connection is a joke.

2.39 Government couldn't produce enough money under FR?

That claim was made by Wray (2014). See paragraph starting "While our governments are large, they are not big enough to provide all the monetary IOUs we need...."

Answer. That contradicts the claim rightly made by Wray and other advocates of MMT, namely that there is NO LIMIT to the amount of money that government can print and spend. Robert Mugabe illustrated that point.

In short, privately produced money is just not necessary.

2.40 FR prevents all lending?

The above bizarre claim is made by De Anglo (2014) and

Bossone (2002).

Answer. Some critics of FR are under the illusion that because FR gives depositors the option of totally safe deposits with relevant sums simply being lodged at the central bank, that therefor no lending takes place under FR. De Angelo (2014) is an example of a paper which (despite all the impressive maths in the paper) makes the latter very elementary blunder.

The notion that under FR, no one can borrow is also trotted out by Bossone.

Bossone's next criticism is thus. (Incidentally notice the near incomprehensible English – much loved by academics).

"In a setting where all individuals are initially identical but learn only subsequently to have different intertemporal consumption preferences, banks are shown to generate liquidity to help individuals who discover to be "patient" consumers to satisfy their needs. They do so by transforming illiquid assets into liquid deposits. This is possible because the averaging out of the withdrawal demands from a large number of depositors allows banks to stabilize their deposit base and transfer deposit ownership without liquidating the assets. From this angle, the social benefit of banking derives from an improvement in risk-sharing, i.e., the increased flexibility of those who have an urgent need to withdraw their funds before the assets mature (Diamond and Dybvig 1986)."

Now what makes Bossone think that under FR households and firms can't borrow, as the above passage implies? The only difference between the existing system and FR is that under the latter, lending is carried out by "banks" or "entities" that are funded just by shareholders, as opposed to the existing system under which lenders are funded mainly by depositors. Indeed, as Bossone himself put it a page or two earlier:

"Commercial banks having to switch to narrow-banking regulation could be expected to transfer their credit exposures to existing or newly-established finance companies, which typically operate with higher capital ratios and fund themselves with relatively larger volumes of long-term debt."

Bossone then repeats the above error (i.e. assuming that no one can borrow under FR) when he says:

"In fact, the benefit of banking cannot be fully appreciated if the asset and the liability side of the bank balance sheet are not considered connectedly. The benefit derives from the banks using their stable deposit base to finance production technologies that increase output over time."

To repeat, under FR, (if we have to use pseudo technical phrases) "production technologies" can be "financed over time" perfectly well under FR.

2.41 Banks will try to circumvent FR rules?

Answer. It is 100% certain that banks would try every trick in the book to circumvent the rules of FR. But then it's a 100% certain they'll try to circumvent ANY RULES or laws. Banks are quasi criminal organisations. The total fines that have been imposed on banks in the US in connection with sundry crimes committed during and before the crisis is in the order of $100bn at the time of writing (yes, that's billion, not million).

But to repeat, at least the rules of full reserve are simple. So to that extent they are easy to enforce.

2.42 Converting to FR involves a huge bailout of existing banks?

Coppola (2012) made the above claim: indeed the title of her article is "Full reserve banking: the largest bank bailout in history."

Answer. The first and obvious flaw in that argument is that the EXISTING BANKING SYSTEM had to be bailed out with trillions of dollars of public money in the crisis or recession which began around 2007. Thus supporters of the existing system are not in a position to preach sermons on "bailouts" to advocates of FR.

A second flaw is that Friedman (1960) advocated FR, and as a staunch advocate of free markets, it is highly unlikely he would have advocated FR had he thought that any sort of "bailout" for private banks was involved.

Incidentally, and as mentioned above, Friedman saw little difficulty in converting to FR. As he put it, *"There is no technical problem in achieving a transition from our present system to 100% reserves easily, fairly speedily and without any serious repercussions on financial or economic markets."*

As to Friedman's use of the word "speedily" he was right to say that the conversion could be done more or less overnight. But to minimise disruption it might well be desirable to convert over a period of months or years. However the BASIC PRINCIPLES involved in both a quick and slow conversion are the same, so it does not matter whether we use a "quick" or "slow" conversion to illustrate the basic principles. But to keep things simple, the quick option is better. So here goes.

A bailout free conversion. Government announces that by a particular point in time, all depositors must allocate their money as between sums they want to be totally safe, and sums they are prepared to put at risk with a view to earning interest (or more interest than is obtainable on the latter totally safe money).

As regards the latter "risk" money, all that is required is to change the description of the money involved. That is, risk money is classified as "stake in a mutual fund" if we adopt Kotlikoff's version of full reserve. Or in the case of PM's system, that money becomes "money in investment accounts". No bailout or anything that faintly resembles a bailout there.

Safe money.

As to money that depositors want to be totally safe, the central bank would need to create and effectively credit those depositors with $X of central bank money for every $X of existing money that those depositors had in commercial banks and which they wanted to be totally safe. And that would be a huge gift to or "bailout" for commercial banks if that was the end of the story. As Coppola put it:

"Under full reserve banking, all banks would have to hold enough funds to allow all sight deposits to be drawn at once. To achieve this, central banks would have to produce a simply ginormous amount of new money: the IMF estimates that for the US, it would be 184% of GDP."

But that is NOT THE END of the story.

What about the loans corresponding to that money? Well that then becomes the property of the central bank. That is, the central bank collects the repayment of capital and interest on those loans till the loans expire. (Incidentally it could easily make sense for commercial banks to collect those repayments of capital and interest ON BEHALF OF the central bank. But that's an administrative detail.)

Coppola evidently didn't grasp the above, that is the fact that in exchange for £Xbn new money, commercial banks simply transfer £Xbn of their assets to the central bank. As she put it:

"Positive Money would no doubt say that as their proposal involves moving transaction accounts from private bank to central bank books, no new money needs to be created. I disagree. In order to move the transaction accounts, the central bank would have to create new reserves to the value of the total balances in those accounts. This is simply a consequence of double entry accounting: it is not possible simply to eliminate deposit balances from private bank balance sheets without also writing off the debt assets that currently back them. So either the central bank must produce new money, or there must be a debt jubilee. (The IMF noticed this and opted for the debt jubilee, but their accounting was

wrong and they didn't consider the inflation consequences of such a massive debt write-off)."

"The IMF" in the latter sentence is a reference to Kumhof (2012). In short, Kumhof made the same mistake as Coppola: neither could see a way of creating the $Xbn of new base money without EITHER making an £$bn gift to commercial banks, OR writing off £$bn of debts owed to commercial banks.

Of course both Coppola and Kumhof are wrong: there is a simple solution to the latter problem, which to repeat, is to transfer $Xbn of commercial bank assets to the central bank.

Small elements of bailout.

There is however a small element of potential bailout if the central bank were to carry any losses arising from repayment of those loans. One possibility there is to simply accept those possible bailout costs as part of the cost for the country as a whole of converting to full reserve.

A second possibility is to get the private sector to insure the central bank against loss. There are always willing buyers of junk bonds and other assets of questionable value.

But it's unlikely that the loss would amount to anything more than a very small proportion of the total of such loans in the case of standard British mortgages. And that accounts for the large majority of lending by banks in the UK.

Moreover, it's near impossible to get the price exactly right when organising a big transfer of assets between public and private sectors or when doing any other type of share offering. For example, with the benefit of hindsight it is now clear that the UK's Post Office was sold to the private sector in 2014 for significantly below a realistic price - £3.6bn too low according to Bloodworth (2014).

2.43 The Money Creation Committee would not regulate demand accurately?

Claimed by Pettifor (2014).

Answer. In a non-FR regime (e.g. the existing system) there is inevitably SOME SORT of committee that takes decisions on stimulus. For example in the UK there is the Bank of England Monetary Policy Committee. Thus the above criticism is no more a criticism of FR / MCCs than of existing and similar committees (whose members are doubtless the first to admit that their economic forecasts are well short of 100% accurate.)

2.44 Interest rate fluctuations would be larger under FR?

Answer. Under FR, at least as proposed by some FR advocates, demand is regulated by adjusting the amount of base money created and spent (net of any changes to tax). Meanwhile, interest rates are left to find their own level. But if that DID result in bigger interest rate fluctuations, that is not a brilliant criticism of FR and for the simple reason that if fluctuations in one part or characteristic of the economy are suppressed or reduced, that will probably just exacerbate fluctuations elsewhere in the economy. In short, if FR does cause increased interest rate fluctuations, that does not prove that the TOTAL AMOUNT of fluctuation in the economy as a whole increases.

For example, if there is an increased demand for loans from businesses and house buyers, in a free market that would raise interest rates. But if the authorities decide to suppress that rise in interest rates by leaving central bank base rates unchanged then commercial banks will simply lend more than if interest rates had risen. And that will raise demand by even more than if interest rates had been allowed to rise.

Now assuming the economy is at capacity / NAIRU, that rise in demand would not be permissible, thus the authorities would have to impose some sort of deflationary measure, like raising taxes or cutting public spending. So in that case, suppressing interest rate fluctuations just results in bigger tax or public spending fluctuations.

Indeed, the inability of the authorities to get the combination of interest rate adjustment and fiscal stimulus right under the existing system was nicely illustrate in Sweden recently. Sweden tried to moderate an asset price bubble by raising interest rates, only to discover that that led to inadequate aggregate demand. See Duxbury (2014).

2.45 Safe banks under FR need subsidies?

George Selgin makes the odd claim that "every significant 100-percent bank known to history was a government-sponsored enterprise, which depended for its existence on some combination of direct government subsidies, compulsory patronage, or laws suppressing rival (fractional reserve) institutions" (Selgin 2011).

Answer. An obvious and very large exception to the latter "universal Selgin law" is the UK's National Savings and Investments, which has been going for over 150 years – though its name has changed a couple of times since it was founded.

NSI is not an absolutely true 100% reserve bank in that it invests mainly in government debt rather than base money. However, government debt and base money merge into each other: that is there is no effective difference between government debt with one week to run till maturity, and base money.

As to the idea that such a bank (a "true" FR bank or an NSI type bank) needs subsidizing, obviously if such a bank invested JUST IN base money, and assuming the central bank paid no interest on such money, then such a bank would need to obtain funds from SOMEWHERE to cover its costs. But does not mean a subsidy is needed: the bank could perfectly well charge depositors for the cost of safeguarding their money. Indeed exactly that scenario has existed over the last three years or so with a significant proportion of current or checking accounts in the UK: that is, the interest paid on that money has been non-existent or way below the cost of administering the account, with the result that a significant proportion of account holders have had to pay for a the privilege of having a current / checking account.

As to Selgin's "compulsory patronage", no sort of force or compulsion has ever been used to get people to open NSI accounts.

And as to his "laws suppressing rival (fractional reserve) institutions", no such suppression has ever been used in the UK to induce people to open accounts at NSI.

Section 3: Flawed arguments FOR full reserve.

3.1 We pay interest on privately created money therefor base money is better.

Answer. This is a complicated issue. The next paragraph below summarises the arguments against the above "base money is better" idea, and that is followed by a more detailed explanation of the point.

Interest is certainly paid on LOANS, whether the loan comes via to a bank or not. As to where BANKS grant loans, that tends not to create money because a loan of $X granted by a bank tends to be matched by deposit/s worth $X, and the latter depositors tend to place their money in term accounts which in turn tend not to be counted as money (except to the extent that banks engage in maturity transformation). In contrast, where a bank so-called "loan" is aimed simply at providing a so called "borrower" with day to day transaction money, no actual loan takes place, though the bank will certainly charge for ADMINISTRATION costs, and will in all probability CALL that charge "interest".

Now for a more detailed explanation of that point.

To illustrate the difference between a bank granting a long term loan and supplying a customer with day to day transaction money, let's imagine that commercial banks set up in what has hitherto been a barter economy, and the banks offer some wondrous new stuff called "money" which disposes of the inefficiencies of barter. (Incidentally "transaction" money in the case of a business is part of the business's so called "working capital").

Citizens open accounts and offer collateral so as to enable their accounts to be credited. And let's assume initially that citizens only want enough money for day to day transactions: i.e. no long term loans are involved.

Now clearly the bank will charge for administration costs (e.g. checking up on the value of collateral). But there is no reason for the bank to charge interest.

Interest is a charge made by a lender for the pain or inconvenience of foregoing consumption (i.e. saving) so that the borrower CAN CONSUME, or "spend". And in creating money out of thin air in our hypothetical economy, the bank has not foregone consumption, and nor has anyone else, so there is no reason to charge interest.

But of course that's not to say that if you get a loan just to give you enough for day to day transactions from a bank that you won't be charged what the bank CALLS interest. The point is that IN REALITY, that charge is for administration costs: it is not genuine interest.

Money creation involves debt creation?

Note also, that where a commercial bank creates just transaction money, no real debt is created. To be more exact, a couple of equal and opposite debts are created (plus a third debt if collateral is deposited). That is, when a bank customer induces a bank to credit $Y to the customer's account, that $Y is a debt owed by the bank to the customer and the customer can force the bank to owe some of that money to whoever the customer chooses using a cheque book, debit card or similar.

But at the same time, the customer, as part of the agreement with their bank undertakes to repay the $Y to the bank at some stage. So there are two equal and opposite debts there. Moreover, if the customer deposits collateral at the bank, then the bank owes that to the customer when the $Y is eventually repaid.

Conclusion so far. Far from money creation by commercial banks involving customers becoming indebted to a bank, there is no net debt either way at the moment the money is created where no collateral is deposited. As to where collateral IS DEPOSITED, the bank is actually in debt to the customer!

Obviously once the customer starts to spend the transaction money, the customer's debt to the bank rises, or where collateral has been deposited, the bank's total or net debt to the customer falls.

Next let us assume that nearly everyone in our hypothetical economy has got themselves some transaction money and we'll assume everyone has an income of some sort (e.g. from work or benefits), the balance on the average customer's bank account will not actually fall at all when the spending starts: what WILL HAPPEN is that the balance bobs up and down.

Obviously it rises when for example the monthly salary is paid, and falls for the rest of the month.

The reason for that is that where one person spends, the relevant money must end up in someone else's bank account. (Incidentally PHYSICAL CASH has been ignored in the above argument, but physical cash forms a very small proportion of the money supply nowadays, so that simplifying assumption is more or less justified.)

Conclusion: when it comes to TRANSACTION money, bank customers pay for ADMINISTRATION COSTS, but they do not pay genuine INTEREST.

Long term loans.

As distinct from supplying transaction money, banks also intermediate between borrowers and lender/savers.

Borrowers don't get loans just to sit a home admiring their newly acquired pile of money: they get loans in order to spend, i.e. consume the fruits of other peoples' labour.

Now the only way to induce anyone to abstain from consumption is for the bank to offer interest to depositors. If interest is offered, then some people will leave more in their bank accounts than they otherwise would. And clearly the bank will have to pass that interest on to borrowers.

In short, banks do not charge interest simply for creating money. But they WILL CHARGE long term borrowers interest, because for every long term loan, there has to be someone making a long term deposit (or a series of people making longish term deposits).

The latter point is not correct in that banks engage in maturity transformation, but that does not greatly detract from the latter point. That is, maturity transformation simply consists of banks lending on money they know perfectly well will not be spent in the next week or month or whatever. And the latter money is a "long term deposit" of a sort. Put another way, where sums are left unused for an extended period in current or checking accounts, that money is effectively a long term loan to a bank rather than money.

Moreover, anyone leaving money in a bank for an extended period, if they have any sense, will put the money in a term account, and money in term accounts tends not to be counted as money, though that depends of course on the length of the "term", i.e. how quickly the customer can get access to their money.

Conclusion. Where banks supply genuine money, that is transaction money, no interest is charged. While as regards long term loans, interest is charged, but little or no money is created. So to the extent that that argument is valid, it is incorrect to say that we pay interest on money issued to us by commercial banks.

3.2 FR benefits the environment and equality.

Claimed by Dyson (2012).

Answer. One can subsidise windfarms (or not) under

fractional reserve, and ditto for full reserve. Plus tax on CO^2 emitting fuels can be raised (or not) under both full and fractional reserve. Thus the environment has little to do with the full versus fractional reserve argument.

It is also hard to see why the PATTERN of consumption would change much give a switch to FR. That is, the proportion of family budgets spent on cars, food, housing, clothes would not change much. Thus there are no obvious environmental effects.

As for inequalities, same applies. FR ought to ameliorate the boom / bust cycle, which in turn would reduce the periods of high unemployment that come after the bust. And that clearly reduces inequalities SOMEWHAT. But there is no obvious reason why equality is an issue that is CLOSELY related to the full versus fractional reserve argument.

3.3 Without debt there would be no money.

I.e. Commercial banks create money when they lend (and thus create debts), thus without debt there would be no money. That is an idea put by Rowbotham (1998).

Answer. The answer to that point is spelled out essentially in section 3.1 just above, that is, when a commercial bank SIMPLY creates money, no long term debt is involved. While in contrast, when a commercial bank grants a long term loan, it can well be argued that little money creation is involved.

3.4 Interest condemns borrowers to perpetual debt.

That is, the money which commercial banks lend out does not supply borrowers with the money to pay interest to said banks, thus, so the argument goes, borrowers are condemned to permanently increasing or never ending debt: an idea put by Rowbotham (1998).

Answer. The flaw in the above point is very simple. It is that interest paid to banks is subsequently returned to households in numerous forms: 1, interest payments by banks to depositors, 2, dividend payments to bank shareholders, 3, payments to bank staff and a large range of other costs that banks have to meet, like upkeep of offices and buying computers.

Of course the latter paragraph blurs the distinction between interest and administration costs somewhat. That distinction is spelled out more clearly in section 3.1 above.

3.5 Full reserve is a huge bonanza for everyone?

The large majority of money is created by commercial banks rather than central banks. It is tempting to deduce from that that were that commercial bank created money produced by the state or central bank instead, that the state would reap the relevant seigniorage profits and would thus be able to spend large additional amounts on health, education and so on. Alternatively taxes could allegedly be reduced by the relevant amount with the result that households would have large additional amounts to spend. That argument is put in a Positive Money article: Positive Money (2013).

The obvious flaw in that argument is that assuming the economy is already at capacity, or nearly so, the above additional spending on various public sector items just won't be possible: excess inflation would ensue if that seigniorage money WERE SPENT.

Alternatively, if the economy is nowhere near capacity, then of course spending the above additional base money WOULD BE STIMULATORY, that is, the additional spending would be beneficial. But the state can create and spend any amount of new base money it likes any time it wants. Thus the above replacement of commercial bank money by state or central bank money does not OF ITSELF achieve anything.

3.6 Fractional reserve banking boosts house prices?

The idea that the existing banking system boosts house prices was put by Dyson (2012, p.126-8). There are four problems with that idea as follows.

1. Other countries have EXACTLY THE SAME banking system as the UK, yet while house prices trebled between 1970 and 2002 in the UK in real terms, there was no increase at all in Germany and Switzerland! At least that's the case according to Evans (2005, p. 23). Incidentally I suspect that "treble" figure is too much: certainly the Economist House Price Index seems to give a slightly lower figure. But that doesn't detract from the basic point which is that if house price increases have been substantially more in the UK than other countries with the same banking system, then it's a near

certainty that it's not the banking system that explains the relatively large house price increase in the UK.

2. The existing or "fractional reserve" banking system has been going for several centuries. There is thus no obvious reason why that banking system has had any more of an effect on house prices in the last ten or twenty years than the last 110 or120 years.

3. If the banking system DOES PROUDCE a bigger demand for houses than would otherwise be the case, that won't result in higher house prices if the supply of stuff needed to build houses (land in particular) is elastic. But of course the supply of land is not elastic, as Evans makes clear. Quite the contrary: in the UK the price of land for building is very restricted. So that's the main explanation for house price increases in the UK.

Dyson claims that extra demand for housing will push up land prices. Well of course it will to a FINITE extent. But given that the price of land where permission has been granted to build houses is about ten times the price of agricultural land, the "Dyson" effect so to speak is near irrelevant. It's pretty obvious that the main reason for the elevated price for land with building permission is that that permission is difficult to get, as Evans makes clear.

4. It is also not true that the fact that banks create money when they make loans has anything to do with house prices. The first problem with that idea is that there is no sharp dividing line between money and non-money. In particular, it is widely accepted around the world that so called money in term accounts does not constitute money where the "term" is

more than about two months. That is, if it takes the depositor longer than about two months to access to their so called money, then what they possess is not really money. Indeed that is a criterion which Dyson himself accepts in that he does not count so called money in the investment accounts he advocates as money where the "term" is sufficiently long.

Now the EXACT amount of money created when a bank grants a loan is very debatable. To the extent that recipients of the new money place it in term accounts of well over two months, then no money is created. But if they place it all in current or checking accounts then new money IS CREATED. And doubtless in the real world the truth or reality lies somewhere between those two extremes. But EXACTLY WHERE "reality" lies is immaterial. Reason is that it's the fact of granting a loan and the relevant money being spent on housing that boosts house prices. Whether that money subsequently boosts the money supply or not makes no difference.

————————

References.

(Most of them being giants whose shoulders I've stood on!)

Note: A large majority of the works below are online and can be accessed via a search engine. In case of any problems, the exact web site addresses are given in the references section of a paper which is an earlier version of this book: it's the Munich Personal RePEc Archive paper No. 57955. The title of the paper is the same as the title of this book.

Admati, A and Hellwig,M, (2013). 'The Bankers' New Clothes: What's Wrong with Banking and What to Do About It'. Princeton University Press.

Admati, A. DeMarzo, P.M., Hellwig, M.F. & Pfleiderer, P. (2013b). 'Fallacies, Irrelevant Facts, and Myths in the Discussion of Capital Regulation: Why Bank Equity is Not Socially Expensive'.

Aziz, J. (2014). 'Prohibition didn't work for liquor — so why ban banking?' The Week.

Bagehot, W. (1873). 'Lombard Street'. Cirencester. The Echo Library.

Bank of England (no date given) 'How Monetary Policy Works'

http://www.bankofengland.co.uk/monetarypolicy/Pages/how.aspx

Birchler, U. & Jackson, P. (2012). 'The Future of Bank Capital.'

Bloodworth, J. (2014). 'Five reasons the Royal Mail should never have been privatised'. Left Foot Forward.

Bossone, B. (2002). 'Should Banks be Narrowed'. Social Science Research Network.

Brown, G. (2013). 'Stumbling Towards the Next Crash'. New York Times.

Bullard, J. (2011). 'Death of a Theory'. Federal Reserve Bank of St. Louis Review.

Cochrane, J. H. (2013). 'Stopping Bank Crises Before They Start'. Hoover Institution, Stanford University.

Coppola, F, (2012). 'Full reserve banking: the largest bank bailout in history'. Coppola Comment.

Coppola, F. (2014). 'Martin Wolf proposes the death of banking'. Pieria.

Corporate Europe Observatory (2014). 'The firepower of the financial lobby'.

CreditCards.com (2009). 'No link between credit card APR and Bank rate, says trade group'.

Darling, A. (2008) 2008A crisis needs a firewall not a ringfence. Financial Times.

De Anglo, H, and Stulz, R. (2014). "Liquid-Claim

Production, Risk Management, and Bank Capital Structure: Why High Leverage is Optimal for Banks". Social Science Research Network.

Diamond, D. & Dybvig, P. (1986). 'Banking Theory, Deposit Insurance and Bank Regulation'. Journal of Business, Vol 59, No.1, pp 55-68.

Dowd, K. (2014) 'Let's not ban private money.' Free Banking.

Duxbury, C. (2014). Sweden's Central bank Cuts Main Interst Rate to Boost Inflation'. Wall Street Journal.

Dyson, B. & Jackson, A. (2012). 'Modernising Money'. Positive Money. London.

Economist (2014) 'Narrow Minded'. The Economist.

Elliot, D.J. (2013). 'Higher Bank Capital Requirements Would Come at a Price'. Brookings Institution.

Evans A.W. & Hartwich, O.M. (2005) 'Unaffordable Housing Fables and Myths'. Policy Exchange.

Fisher, I. (1936) '100% Money and the Public Debt'. Michael Schemmann.

Fisher, R. (2013). 'Ending 'Too Big to Fail': A Proposal for Reform Before It's Too Late.'

Friedman, M. (1960). 'A Program for Monetary Stability.' New York. Fordham University Press.

Greenspan, A. (2014). 'Greenspan (2014) says bubbles can't be stopped without crunch'. Market Watch.

Haldane, A.G. (2013). Have we solved 'too big to fail'? Vox.

Hillinger, C (2010) 'The Crisis and Beyond'. Economics, Discussion Paper No. 2010-23.

Insley, J. (2011). 'Credit card interest rates hit 13-year high, analysis shows.' The Guardian, London.

Johnson, D. S., J. A. Parker, and N. S. Souleles (2006). 'Household expenditure and the income tax rebates of 2001'. The American Economic Review 96.

Kashyap, A.K., Stein, J.C. & Hanson, S. (2010). 'An Analysis of the Impact of "Substantially Heightened" CapitalRequirements on Large Financial Institutions'.

Kay, J. (2009) 'Narrow Banking: The Reform of Banking Regulation'. Centre for the Study of Financial Innovation.

King, M. (2010) 'Banking from Bagehot to Basel and Back Again.' Second Bagehot Lecture given at the Buttonwood Gathering, New York City.

Klein, M, (2013). 'The Best Way to Save Banking Is to Kill It.', Bloomberg.

Kotlikoff, L. (2012). The Economic Consequences of the Vickers Commission. London. Civitas.

Kregel, J. (2012). 'Minsky and the narrow banking proposal.' Levy Economics Institute of Bard College, Public

Policy Brief, No.125, 2012.

Krugman, P. (2014). 'Is a Banking Ban the Answer?' New York Times.

Krugman, P (2014b). 'Good News on Financial Reform' New York Times.

Kumhof, M. & Benes, J. (2012). 'The Chicago Plan Revisited'. IMF working paper.

Miles, D., Yang J., and Marcheggiano G. (2011). 'Optimal Bank Capital'. Bank of England External MPC Unit Discussion paper No.31. Note: the version of this paper referred to here is the April 2011 version, not the January 2011 version.

Miller, M. (1995). 'Do the M&M propositions apply to banks'. Journal of Banking and Finance, 19 (1995) 483-489.

Mathaison, N., Newman, & McClenaghan, M. (2012). 'Revealed: The £93m City lobby machine'. Bureau of Investigative Journalism.

O'Brien, E. (2014). 'N.Z. Labour to Make Central Bank Law Change in First Term.' Bloomberg.

Peston, R. (2012). 'How do we fix this mess'. Hodder & Stoughton.

Pettifor, A. (2014). 'Why I disagree with Martin Wolf and Positive Money'.

Positive Money (2013). 'Taxes and Public Spending'.

Ratnovski, L. (2013). 'How much Capital Should Banks Have?' Voxeu.

Rowbotham, M. (1998). 'The Grip of Death.' Jon Carpenter, Oxfordshire.

Ryan-Collins, J, Greenham, T, Bernardo, G. and Werner, R. (2013). 'Strategic Quantitative Easing', New Economics Foundation.

Schiller, R. (2014). 'The Financial Fire Next Time.' Project Syndicate.

Schoder, C. (2013). 'Credit vs. demand constraints: The determinants of US firm-level investment over the business cycles from 1977 to 2011.' The North American Journal of Economics and Finance.

SEC (2014). '17 CFR Parts 230, 239, 270, 274 and 279 Release No. 33-9616.

Selgin, G. (1988). 'The Theory of Free Banking' Lanham. Rowman & Littlefield.

Selgin, G. (2012). 'Is Fractional Reserve Banking Inflationary?' Capitalism Magazine.

Selgin, G. (2011) 'The State and 100 percent Reserve Banking'. Free Banking.

Sharpe, S.A. & Suarez, G.A. (2014). 'The insensitivity of investment to interest rates: Evidence from a survey of

CFOs.'

Tobin, J. (1985). 'Financial Innovation and Deregulation in Perspective'.

Tobin, J. (1987) 'The case for preserving regulatory distinctions'.

Turner, A. (2010). 'What Do Banks Do?' in 'The Future of Finance'. London School of Economics.

Turner, A. (2014). 'Escaping the debt addiction. Monetary and macro prudential policy in the post crisis world'. Centre for Financial Studies, Frankfurt.

Turner, A. (2012). 'Monetary and Financial Stability: Lessons from the Crisis and from classic economics texts'. Speech at South African Reserve Bank.

UK CreditCards.com (2009) 'No link between credit card APR and Bank rate, says trade group'.

Van Dixhoorn, C. (2013). 'Full Reserve Banking'. Sustainable Finance Lab.

Vickers, J. (2011). Independent Commission on Banking Final Report.

Warner, J. (2014). 'Bankers have done a good job of creating money.' London. Daily Telegraph.

Weiner, K. (2014). 'Will Nw Money Market Rules Break Money Markets?' Forbes.

Werner, R. A. (1997). 'Towards a New Monetary Paradigm: a Quantity Theorem of Disaggregated Credit, with Evidence from Japan.' Kredit und Kapital, vol. 30, no. 2, pp. 276---309, Berlin: Duncker und Humblot.

Werner, R., A. (2005). 'New Paradigm in Macroeconomics: Solving the Riddle of Japanese Macroeconomic Performance'. Basingstoke: Palgrave Macmillan. 38.

Werner, R., Dyson, B. Greenham, T. Ryan-Collins, J., (2011). 'Towards A Twenty---first Century Banking And Monetary System.' Positive Money, NEF and the University of Southampton Submission to the Independent Commission on Banking.

Wolf, M. (2012)' 'Seven ways to clean up our banking cesspit.' London. Financial Times. (July 12).

White, L.H. (2003)' 'Accounting for Fractional-Reserve Banknotes and Deposits—or, What's Twenty Quid to the Bloody Midland Bank?' Independent Review, Vol 7, No.3, Winter 2003.

Wolf, M. (2013)' 'Why bankers are intellectually naked.' Financial Times.

Wray, L.R. (2014). 'Modern Monetary Theory: The Basics'.

Wren-Lewis, S. & Portes, J. (2014) 'Issues in the Design of Fiscal Policy Rules'. University of Oxford Department of Economics discussion paper 704

Wren-Lewis, S. (2013). 'Why the Pigou Effect does not get you out of a liquidity trap'. Mainly macro.

Wren-Lewis, S. (2014b). 'Time inconsistency and debt'.